# Contents

# Gratitude

If I have seen further than others, it is by standing upon the shoulders of giants.

**– Sir Issac Newton**

The ideas in this book are partly a fusion of the transformational conversations I have had with my mentors, teachers & friends. I would like to start by expressing my gratitude towards mentors & teachers. They have served as my beacon of light.

My heartfelt thank you to Ms. Archana Parikh for the life transforming impact she has had on my life. Her contribution in helping me through the whole process of the book has been immense & vital.

I am indebted to Mr. Anil Pereira for imbibing in me the philosophy of improving the processes, irrespective of the outcome.

My sincere thanks to Mr. Sandeep Biswal for shaping my career with his unconditional support & the impactful conversations.

I express my deep gratitude towards Mr. G Ramesh Babu, Late Mrs. Vijaya Promod, Mr. Prabhakar, Mr. Murty CM,

Mr. Arun Nadar, Mr. Manikandan AVM & Ms. Vadivukkarasi Gunasundari for believing in me.

I am in gratitude to my friends Ankit, Bibhor, Salil, Shreyash, Siddharth & Subhaj for the deep & engaging conversations and encouragement that inspired me to write this book.

My deepest gratitude and pranaam to my Dadi, Mummy and Maa for instilling in me the love for stories and nurturing my curiosity.

In complete gratitude to my Dada, Papa & Baba for imprinting in me the right values and the attitude to never give up.

To my greatest cheerleader and better half Ritu, for her unwavering support throughout.

To my sister Srishti for her unconditional encouragement.

To my brother Dr. Vivek Shankar for his unequivocal support.

Last but not the least, I thank Santosh Bhaiya for the profound impact he has had on my formal as well as experiential education right from my first day at school.

# Foreword

In an era where career choices resemble a lavish menu rather than a simple selection, Shrey embarks on a journey to demystify the daunting task of career selection. As someone who witnessed the transition from limited options to an overwhelming array, Shrey brings a refreshing perspective to the table.

With astute observation, a profound understanding of psychology, and extensive experience in Learning & Development and Talent Management, Shrey presents a compelling framework tailored to align careers with individual personalities. His approach, articulated through engaging fictional conversations, captures the essence of mentorship and pays homage to the timeless Guru-Shishya tradition.

In this book, Shrey doesn't promise wealth, but he offers something more profound—a pathway to fulfillment. By embracing his framework, readers can navigate the complexities of the professional world with confidence and authenticity.

I have no doubt that Shrey's work will stand the test of time, becoming a cornerstone in the realm of career guidance. Through his insights, he empowers individuals to shape their destinies and create lives enriched with purpose and meaning.

Prepare to embark on a transformative journey—one that promises not just success, but a deeper connection to one's true calling. Shrey's wisdom will undoubtedly leave an indelible mark on those who dare to explore its depths.

– Padma Shri Anand Kumar, Founder and Inspiration of Super 30 Program and Movie.

# Preface

In my journey through life, I've always harboured a relentless curiosity about the underlying reasons behind the things I'm passionate about. One such enigma that has long intrigued me is the concept of Career. I've often pondered why some individuals approach their careers with fervent zeal while others merely view it as a means to an end. This curiosity ignited a quest within me—an exploration into the essence of Career Passion.

As I delved deeper into this inquiry, it unfurled a myriad of interconnected questions:

Why do certain professions command higher salaries than others?

What factors contribute to the perceived importance of one job over another?

Which skills endure the test of time, and which ones fade into obsolescence?

How does one navigate the labyrinthine path to their dream career?

And, perhaps most crucially, how does one even identify their dream career amidst a sea of options?

This book is my earnest endeavor to unravel these mysteries by presenting my insights through the lens of mental models

I've meticulously crafted and refined over time. These models are a culmination of my personal reflections and opinions, narrated through the veil of fiction. While the characters and scenarios within these pages are fictitious, the underlying principles are rooted in the fabric of reality.

Over the span of more than a decade, across diverse professional roles—particularly my tenure as the Head of Learning and Development at Visible Alpha, and my involvement in Talent Management—I've been afforded a privileged vantage point to observe and analyze the intricacies of the career landscape. Drawing from these experiences, coupled with an understanding of personality types, the psychology of motivation, and the stark realities of the professional world, I've crafted mental frameworks to decipher the enigmatic world of careers.

I'm a firm believer in the continuous refinement of my mental models. While I strive to solidify them through logical scrutiny and empirical evidence, I remain open to new perspectives and feedback from real-world applications. This book encapsulates my current truth, but I acknowledge the potential for evolution and growth. Should my insights evolve, I pledge to revise this work accordingly, ensuring its resonance with the ever-shifting dynamics of the career sphere.

It is my sincerest hope that you glean valuable insights from these pages, empowering you to navigate your career journey with clarity and purpose. And if you find this book beneficial, I urge you to pay it forward, sharing the wisdom with others who may benefit from its teachings.

Wishing you enlightenment and fulfillment on your career odyssey.

# Chapter 1

# Serendipity

"May I have your attention, please? Train no 17884, Puri Nizamuddin Kalinga Utkal express is arriving shortly at platform no 3."

Hearing the announcement, Tushar was ecstatic. The train was on time & the vacation he was waiting for months was about to begin shortly. The train journey made him nostalgic about his college days. It reminded him of the piping hot tea, samosas, and lively conversations with complete strangers.

The resounding horn of the train brought him back to the present moment. The train finally halted. He quickly picked his backpack and embarked. He had booked a side upper berth in a 3AC compartment. The side upper was a well-thought bet. If he found a co-passenger, he could sit and converse, and if luck did not favor him he always had the option to retire to his solitude. He swiftly placed his backpack under the seat and took his seat.

He was heading to Puri, the abode of Lord Jagarnath. Apart from being a spiritual center, Puri is known to have clean beaches & has many tourist destinations close by like Konark, Dhauli Giri etc. The Odisha government had transformed it over the years into a quality tourist destination.

Tushar started to wonder, I have been looking forward to this vacation for months now. To be honest, as much as I am excited about the vacation,I am also relieved to escape the constant stress of my 9 to 6 job life. A life that has a lot of promise with accompanying perks & benefits but is barely fulfilling.

It had been barely a year since Tushar had started working. He was so excited about the job. He had thought he would get to apply all he had learned in his college & go from strength to strength. He believed work would be fun & he would tap dance to work. But the gap between his expectation & reality was massive. He found his job to provide barely any ground to apply what he had learned in college. He had a standard process that he had to follow. Any deviation from it would reduce his efficiency & hence his output. The time bound targets that he had to meet ensured he only followed the standard procedure. All this caused him a lot of stress. It wasn't that he did not try to enjoy it, he did do so by having a constructive approach, attempting to see how the impact of his work fit in the larger scheme of things. But the monotony & lack of scope for experimentation made him feel trapped. Forget tap dancing to work, getting himself out of his bed, to go to work had become a task. He had begun to doubt his potential

He would often think, Am I the only one who is feeling so disconnected with my work? Am I not good enough? Am I being a pessimist? Will I ever get to put my skills to application? Will I ever enjoy my work?

"Do you mind if I use your charging port?"

The question jolted Tushar out of his thoughts. He involuntarily replied, "Yes."

The voice replied, "Thanks! I appreciate it!"

He turned around & saw a middle aged man, who would have been in his late 30s. He was wearing a light pink linen shirt with sleeves folded & cream trousers. He wore a classic analog watch & had an air of simplicity. Yet his voice was griping.

The man settled down in his seat & introduced himself,

"Hi, I am Chanakya. I am traveling to Bhubaneshwar. What about you?"

"Hi Chanakya, I am Tushar. I am traveling to Puri." Replied Tushar

"Oh Puri! It's a beautiful city." Replied Chanakya.

"I am sure it is," Tushar said.

"What takes you to Puri?", asked Chanakya.

"I am going for a vacation." Replied Tushar

"That's great! Puri is a place with an auspicious shrine, a clean & beautiful beach & a lot of important historical places around. I am sure you are going to have a good time!" said Chanakya.

"I hope so." Tushar replied.

"Between, what takes you to Bhubaneshwar?" Tushar asked.

"I am going there to conduct career workshops." Replied Chanakya.

"That sounds interesting. What is it that you do?" Tushar asked.

"I am a Career Mentor, I help people choose a career aligned to their personality." Replied Chanakya.

"Wow! That reminds me of 3 idiots!"[1] "Farhan chose to be a wildlife photographer instead of an engineer. But I thought that only happens in movies." said Tushar.

"Ha ha, well it can happen in your life too. Conscious choice is all you would need to make & you can tap dance to work!" Said Chanakya.

'Tap dance to work!' Tushar wondered.

"Well that definitely sounds ambitious. Can it really happen to everyone in their career or is it for a select few like Sachin Tendulkar, Warren Buffett etc?" Tushar asked.

Chanakya smiled & said, "it can happen to anyone. I have implemented it in my work-life & helped many over the years implement it in theirs & our work lives have undergone a transformation. It takes some effort & time, but if you get the process right & stay put, the proceeds eventually follow."

---

1. Reference: 3 Idiots (2009) hindi movie.

"Process & Proceeds big words," Tushar couldn't stop & rhetorically remarked  in a sarcastic manner.

"I understand where you are coming from. You are not the first person to react like this on this topic. The reason is very few people without any conscious effort land up in careers aligned to their personality," said Chanakya.

They were interrupted by the pantry boy, who had come to take the order for lunch. Both Chanakya & Tushar ordered for a veg thali. The interruption made Tushar conscious about his sarcastic remark. He felt guilty about his spontaneous reaction.

"I am sorry for the remark. But I am speaking out of the experience I have had. I agree with your statement about few people being in the career they are meant for, now that I think of it. To be honest, I have never had a chance to think about it at a collective level. I have been too caught up and struggling to figure out my own work life. Can you help me understand why it happens?" said Tushar.

"I can understand. Let's first try and understand it at an individual level & then we will think about the group level. Would you be comfortable sharing about your education and your own work-life?" Asked Chanakya.

Usually Tushar was a reserved person, who would open up gradually. But Chanakya's simple, down to earth & understanding demeanor put Tushar at ease and he was willing to share.

Tushar briefed Chanakya about how excited he was when he had joined this role as the first job after his MBA in Finance. He stated how excited he was to apply all that he had learned in his MBA course. He spoke about how excited he was to make key decisions & test his theories through application. He spoke about the mismatch in his expectations & reality. He narrated his frustration with standard operating procedures & tight timelines. He narrated how he felt being treated like a mechanical machine by his superiors. He finally revealed how all this had led him into doubting his potential.

It was the first time Tushar had spoken about what he was going through in his work life to anyone. He felt relieved and out of breath.

Chanakya comforted Tushar by giving him some water. Tushar settled down after a while & looked at Chanakya with hope & curiosity.

Chanakya began, "The pressures of modern day life to get placed, earn well, buy a house, buy a car, settle down with a purpose of leading a happy & peaceful life, in all of this it's the work life that takes the hit. The job market becomes a corporate's market, where for an extra few lakhs in annual package, there are swarms of people who are willing to take up any career without any thought to whether they would enjoy it in the first place or not. This makes our work life the epicenter of our unhappiness & percolates to other areas of our life defeating the whole purpose of leading a happy & peaceful life. It's not that people can't understand this and make better choices, it's just that the environment & lack of guidance makes people walk this path in a herd. So, I can relate to what you are going through & I empathize with you. Before we discuss further. I would like to first put your self doubt to rest. For now just trust me & believe in yourself & your potential".

"Thank you for the much needed encouragement", said Tushar.

"Now that we have the problem at hand let's try and break down the problem.

I see 3 key parts:

1.  Your job role

2.  Your expectation

3.  Your manager

We will elaborate on each of them individually, starting with your Job role".

"To understand your current job role & figuring out the career that would best suit you we will need a thorough understanding of the following questions":

1.  Who are you as a person? What's your natural strength?

2.  What do you aspire to become & why?

3.  What are the important parameters across which a career needs to be evaluated? How do different careers stack across these important parameters?

4. How do you pick the best career aligned to yourself, your strengths, your aspirations & your motivations?

5. How would you transition from your current career to your desired career?

6. What are the roadblocks one faces that hinder people from realizing their dream career?

"That sounds a lot", said Tushar.

"It's a framework that might appear overwhelming to you written as a checklist. But by the time we complete our discussion, I assure you, you will be able to play with it like a Rubik cube. Are you willing to be patient?", asked Chanakya.

"If that's the case I am all ears", replied Tushar enthusiastically.

# Chapter 2

# Understanding Yourself With Your Strengths

It was lunch time already & the pantry boy had just delivered the food. The intense conversation had left both Chanakya & Tushar feeling hungry. They enjoyed their lunch, it was reasonably filling. Then each of them took a walk turn by turn, so as to keep an eye on their belongings. They then resumed the conversation. Tushar initiated it with a question that had popped up in his head.

"Sir, Do dream careers exist?", asked Tushar

Chanakya replied with a cheeky smile, "No they don't, but you can always create them."

Tushar was perplexed and asked, "What do you mean?'

"What I mean is, most of the time we do not start off with a dream career, but gradually evolve towards it as we progress". explained Chanakya.

"Okay. That sounds plausible", replied Tushar.

Tushar was struck by a thought, it means there was still hope for him to evolve into a career that he dreamed of.

With the renewed surge of energy brought on by the hope of a fulfilling career, Tushar asked enthusiastically, "Can you elaborate, how to evolve into a dream career?"

Chanakya was pleased to see the childlike enthusiasm & hope in Tushar's demeanor. In a calming voice Chanakya said, "I can feel your enthusiasm & hopefulness, but let's go in a step by step manner, so that you understand the framework completely. We will cover this when we answer, How to transition from your current career to your desired career? For now let's come back to exploring our first question - which is, Who are you as a person? What's your natural strength?"

Tushar thought for a good 15 minutes and replied, "I know who I am and what my strengths are generally. But I don't know what is relevant to our context exactly and what's not."

Chanakya replied, "Good!"

Tushar was confused again.

Chanakya said, "The beginning of any learning is acceptance & confusion is the mother of intelligence."

Tushar still had the perplexed expression on his face.

Chanakya elaborated, "Let's understand each question in a step by step manner keeping in mind the context of the discussion."

Chanakya continued,[2] "Do you identify yourself as an Introvert or an Extrovert?"

Tushar immediately replied, "Extrovert."

"Are you sure?", checked Chanakya.

"Ya I have good people skills, so that makes me an Extrovert."

Chanakya smiled & said, "That's inconclusive a reason to call yourself an Extrovert."

Tushar did not know what to say.

Chanakya proceeded, "When I say Extrovert or Introvert, what I mean is, where do you draw your energy from, your internal world or your me-time versus your external world or interactions with people."

Tushar paused for a moment and then replied, "Both. I sometimes prefer me-time and on other occasions I prefer interactions with people."

Chanakya smiled and said, "That's good" and asked, "What do you prefer when you are drained?"

Tushar immediately replied, "me-time."

"Bingo that explains. You are more inclined towards Introversion", explained Chanakya.

Tushar refuted, "But I have excellent people skills."

---

2. Is inspired from Myers–Briggs Type Indicator, a type of personality test.

Chanakya asked,[3] "Who said an introvert cannot have good people skills?"

Tushar was bowled again.

Chanakya explained further, "Actually Introversion & Extroversion are not binary, but a continuous spectrum and we all fall somewhere in between. In your case Introversion is dominant as you prefer me-time when you are drained, which is when you are most likely to be your truest self."

Tushar had a revelation. He was enjoying the conversation to the fullest. He was eager to find the end framework, yet at the same time was loving the exploratory conversation.

Though Tushar did not say it out loud, his expressions were clearly indicating the same for Chanakya, who had the eye to read nonverbal cues.

Chanakya continued, "Do you trust something when you can imagine or do you trust only when you see it tangibly? Which of them is your default method?"

Tushar thought for a while again and began to speak, "Though I am good with data analysis, I trust something when I can imagine it and the dots connect in my head."

"And how often do you act on your trust?", asked Chanakya cheekily.

"Sometimes", replied Tushar coyly.

---

3. Is inspired from Myers–Briggs Type Indicator, a type of personality test.

"Well then you should back your belief more often, young man," said Chanakya in a firm & encouraging voice.[4]

Tushar nodded in agreement.

Chanakya concluded, "So you are more inclined towards connecting the dots kind of processing, also known as intuitive processing, opposed to touch & feel, also called sensory processing."

"Is this a continuous spectrum?", Tushar quickly asked.

"Yes, most of the opposites in the world are a continuous spectrum in practice, quite opposite to theory", added Chanakya.

"That's a rare insight", complimented Tushar.

Moving ahead, "Do you make decisions after consciously weighing the pros & cons or how you feel about the people involved or the situation?", asked Chanakya.

Tushar responded in a meek voice, "By now you know I am guilty of being driven by feelings."

"That's nothing to be ashamed of. Our feelings are a result of evolution, just like our intuition and often lead us to better decisions compared to decisions arrived only with conscious thinking done with a limited data. The only thing that can distort our feelings is our biases that are a result of our experiences, especially pronounced experiences", said Chanakya

---

4. Is inspired from Myers–Briggs Type Indicator, a type of personality test.

"That's a unique perspective of looking at feelings. I already feel so much better'" Said Tushar, beaming a smile. [5]

He then asked, "But tell me something, is there anyone who is a complete thinker?"

"Acharya Chanakya", replied Chanakya with a wink.

Both of them burst out laughing calling out the historical coincidence.

Chanakya in a reverberating voice recited, "There are no accidents!"

They had a hearty laugh again.

Jokes apart, "thinking & feeling too is a continuous spectrum and you lean towards feeling more", Said Chanakya

Now let's understand: "Are you an organized or a spontaneous person?" asked Chanakya

"I am fairly organized. Sometimes to the extent that I am touted to have OCD towards organization. I personally don't think that's true, I do have scope for spontaneity within my scheduled time, but yes the point is within the scheduled time", said Tushar thoughtfully.

"Fair enough. Then in this spectrum of organization to spontaneity, you are more inclined towards organization", confirmed Chanakya

---

5. Is inspired from Myers–Briggs Type Indicator, a type of personality test.

"That's all we need to understand your personality from a career standpoint", concluded Chanakya.[6]

"Now let's understand your strengths. What is it that you were the best at, irrespective of who you competed against?", asked Chanakya.

"Think of every activity, irrespective of the importance of the activity & figure out what is a competitive advantage you have had that would help you ace anyone. It could be anything from finding hidden things, to selling, to painting, or dancing, or maybe spotting errors etc." added Chanakya.

"Take some time to review your whole life in your head, there is no hurry. You have the next couple of hours, while I take a nap", added Chanakya and laid on his bed, refreshed himself and retired for an afternoon nap.

Tushar in the meantime reviewed memories of his entire life sitting by the window watching trees pass by & sipping a cup of hot coffee. He went through his memories systematically like a query running through a database. He expanded everything that he felt was significant and noted it on a piece of paper that he had borrowed from the pantry boy who came to take their order for dinner. He reviewed his memory chronologically starting from whatever he remembered from his early childhood, his primary school days followed by his high school days, the phase when he prepared for competitive exams and took a one year drop, his college life and his recent work life. He did find a few occasions where he felt he had a certain midas touch in the

---

6. Is inspired from Myers–Briggs Type Indicator, a type of personality test.

way he used his skills to deal seamlessly with certain tricky situations. He could sense a vague sort of pattern emerge, but was not sure what to call the skill exactly, as it was a combination of the ability to analyze a situation & develop an understanding of the context quickly, with the ability to see a situation as part of a pattern and come up with an effective solution. He needed Chanakya's help to crystalize the pattern and map it to the exact skills.

Tushar thought to himself, this exercise of reviewing his whole life with the intent of finding his strength that gave him an edge over others was the first of its kind that he had undertaken. It made him see hope through all the small victories he had over the years, as he re-lived each one by one. In fact some instances were even daily events, which he had never considered to be of any material importance ever. Yet today when he was thinking through, he could see how he had used his skills like a monk using a kung-fu maneuver. It lifted his spirits and made him feel positive about himself, as if he was special. He wanted to stay in this newly found happy mind-space & explore it well to understand himself better.

"Good evening!", said Chanakya

Tushar was shaken out of his deep reverie, looking up with his lit up eyes he said, "Finally! a very good evening!" Tushar had been waiting to share his findings with Chanakya.

"I will need a cup of tea to reboot", said Chanakya.

"The tea vendors have been frequent. We should have one soon".

"I was hoping to get a special tea, the one that you get at stations", said Chanakya out aloud.

"We will reach Gwalior station in 15 minutes, You can get good tea there", a co-passenger sitting adjacent to our seat said.

"Thank you! That's amazing!" replied Chanakya.

Soon we were at the tea stall on Gwalior station, sipping piping hot tea. The tea was indeed special!

The climate was pleasant. We strolled the platform and bought a few eatables.

Tushar felt as if his batteries had been recharged without the usual recharge methods. Just thinking about our strengths and understanding who we are, can have such a positive impact on us. I had heard this, but I experienced it today, thought Tushar as he strolled the platform with spring in his stride.

Soon they heard the siren, boarded their coach and settled comfortably in their seats.

Tushar could not wait any longer and hurriedly asked, "Can we move our conversation ahead?"

"Ofcourse, someone seems to be in a hurry and seems to have hit a jackpot running horses in the memory lane", replied Chanakya cheekily.

"Seems so to me too", Tushar said in agreement.

Tushar quickly added, "After reviewing my memory I have come to a conclusion that my skill sets are a combination of the ability to analyze a situation & develop an understanding of the key moving parts of the context quickly & the ability to see a situation as part of a pattern. Both of them have helped come up with an effective solution & produce maverick-like outcomes."

Chanakya had an expression of amazement on his face and said, "You seem to have done some quality contemplation to reach those conclusions. Commendable!"

"Thank you, but I am unable to condense it further. Can you help me?", asked Tushar.

"Sure I would love to. But before we do that. Can you elaborate on the instances in your life where you used these skill sets?", asked Chanakya.

"Absolutely, let me go one by one."

"The first major instance I can recall is from my class 10th when I was representing my school in a prestigious cricket tournament. We were playing the semi-finals and were pitted against Academia School, a side that had 2 Ranji trophy probables playing for them. It was a 20 over match and we won the toss. We batted first and put up an average score of 96 that we had to defend. I was the opening bowler. I am a left-arm fast bowler. The lad facing the bowling was a Ranji trophy probable and was the best batsman of the side. His name was Sanat."

My captain had told me the previous night, if I could get Sanat's wicket, I would get a biryani treat. I had been observing him from the beginning of the match. Sanat was a right arm fast bowler and bowled at a very good pace for the age group of under-16. He took 3 wickets in his first 3 overs while giving 5 runs, but went for 12 runs in his 4th over without any wickets. The over gave me a peek into his mind. We had our best hitter, Kartik bat during that over. Sanat bowled the first ball and it was a perfect good length delivery with good carry outside off-stump. Kartik missed the delivery completely, as it was too fast for what he was used to facing. Sanat bowled the next ball at middle stump line. This time around Kartik's reaction was better, but he still missed it. The ball was pitched above the stumps and missed everything to be collected by the wicket-keeper. Then Sanat tried going for the kill and tried a yorker, which due to poor execution turned out to be over pitched delivery on the bat. By then Kartik's eyes were set. He drove it past mid-on for 4. The next 3 balls too were over pitched deliveries. Kartik capitalized on 3 of them and got 3 fours, one was through covers, another through mid-wicket and the final one of the pads through backward point. The whole episode told me one thing, Sanat had practiced his stock deliveries to perfection, but once he became overconfident, he tried new things and that is where the chink in the armour was.

I bowled my first delivery; it was a typical left-armers delivery pitching on middle stump and shaping out with the angle. I had knowingly kept the pace below my average speed & bowled it with no swing to provoke Sanat. Sanat, who had taken a middle stump guard, took a stride forward and comfortably defended it. I replicated the first delivery; the result was the same. Now before the 3rd delivery, he changed his guard to a leg-stump guard. Probably to make the room required to play flat batted shorts. A leg stump guard is usually a very aggressive guard. Also, flat batted shorts are stuff of hitters and are not advised to be played, especially when the ball is still new. I understood he was going out of his perfection territory into an aggressive zone and was likely to make a mistake. The gully fielder, Azhar, came up to me and confirmed my hunch. He said Sanat turned around and signaled his team. He was going to be aggressive. I had understood the context, picked the pattern and got my confirmation. I executed my plan perfectly. To get the best shine, I rubbed the ball. I put all I could in the delivery and bowled it with my highest level of skill for an outswinger pitching on leg-stump and swung sharply away towards 1st slip. Sanat played a premeditated cover drive. The pace and swing of the delivery surprised him. He was not in control of the shot. The ball kissed his blade and the gully fielder took an outstanding catch.

Chanakya exclaimed, "Quite an insight and outstanding execution!"

"It is one of my biggest achievements personally", said Tushar.

"I haven't seen you play, but going by your account, I can infer you study your opponents well!", said Chanakya

"Some people use more of their physical muscle to overcome a situation. I just choose to use my mental muscles more", said Tushar.

"Hmm. Interesting! Let's hear your other memories", suggested Chanakya.

Tushar continued, "Sure."

"Recently we had a data conference where a lot of our target customers would be visiting. Our company was participating to demonstrate our data platform and generate traction & potential sales for our platform. I had volunteered to be in the organizing team. There were stalls outside the conference room for sponsors. The sponsors had 3 categories: Platinum, Gold & Silver costing Rs.12 lakhs, Rs.5 lakhs & Rs.3 lakhs respectively. Platinum sponsors got the best located stalls, just outside the conference room. Gold sponsors got the stall that was a little away, but was in the proximity. Silver sponsors got the farthest placed stall near the dining hall. The organizing team had a discussion with the founder and decided to shell out Rs.5 lakhs, but were not too happy with the location of the stalls. An idea struck me, but I wanted to get a feel of the venue. So, I visited the venue over the weekend and studied the locations. Next Monday, I suggested that we have the stall at the entrance of the dining hall. The stall cost a sponsorship of Rs.3 lakhs. My organizing teammates were confused. I explained, irrespective of who's who, everyone is going to have lunch. Which means they would inevitably pass our stall. If we could get a screen to play a video demonstrating our analytics platform, we could get traction as good as the Platinum sponsor stalls and maybe even better. My team supported the idea, and we were on the execution in no time. The screen rent cost us an extra Rs.15 thousand. The conference turned out to be a huge traction generator and got us many sales leads. Everyone appreciated me for the ingenious idea", Tushar added.

Chanakya seemed impressed!

He said, "Indeed a simple yet powerful insight that you capitalized on!"

"Thank you", said Tushar.

"Would these stories suffice to move further with the process?" asked Tushar.

"Yes, I think we have enough context to move ahead", replied Chanakya.

"Great! I am all ears to know your understanding. I have broadly figured, it is something to do with my analytical skill, but I think there is more to it than meets my eyes." said Tushar.

Chanakya started, "Analytical skill is a pretty broad term. There are finer nuances, like you said. Let's explore them."

"In both situations, you were able to identify the key drivers of the existing situation. Once you had the key drivers of the existing situation, you were able to match it to a pre-existing pattern you had in your memory. Based on the above you were able to plan your course of action to win the situation again by leveraging on lessons from solutions that were used in earlier instances in your memory. Does this sound similar to what goes on in your head?"

Tushar was listening to Chanakya intently. He took a deep breath, followed it with a long pause filled with self-reflection. Once he gathered his thoughts, he spoke, "To be honest, I had never thought of it this way before. But now when I think about it, it makes so much sense".

"In the first instance, I had an insight. Sanat was near perfect in what he had practiced. That was bowling a good length delivery and conventional batting. But the moment he ventured into experimenting, he was more likely to make a mistake. I had seen this pattern over and over again in international cricket."

"Sachin Tendulkar, the Maestro, would do it often with ease. For instance, in one of the India vs Australia matches during the ICC Champions Trophy 2000, Sachin read the conditions and found them favorable for seam bowling. If he let McGrath bowl to his natural strength, India, who was put into bat, could get into deep trouble. So, Sachin got McGrath to leave his perfect line & length by instigating him. McGrath was near perfect with bowling to his strengths, but outside his circle of competence whenever he ventured, he was likely to make a mistake. Exploiting the same Sachin got India to a flying start."

"For the solution, I picked what Wasim Akram had done to dismiss Rahul Dravid during an India vs Pakistan test match; He bowled a couple of in-singer to Dravid and then a brilliant out-swinger that moved from leg-stump, kissed the bat, the off-stump and was collected by the wicketkeeper."

"So yes, in this situation I picked the key driver, which was figuring out what came in Sanat's circle of competence and what didn't. I immediately matched the pattern of his venturing out of his circle of competence, leading to him being more vulnerable. I confirmed the same with my observation of his bowling, where he went for 3 boundaries in a row, venturing out of his circle of competence. I executed a couple of in-swinger & one out-swinger trap and added variation of pace to get Sanat to become overconfident and venture out of his circle of competence."

"Well attributed analysis! Let's hear your attribution analysis for the second instance", exclaimed Chanakya.

"Yes, I am enjoying this!" said Tushar.

Tushar continued,

"I had always seen credit card sales agents at the entry of the mall and at airports. I had checked with them about their rentals and learned that they pay a handsome rent for the spot. This was because these spots gave them assured traction that could be converted to potential sales. Another pattern that I had formed was the importance of appealing visual display. The Drishyam movie reinforces this pattern. The movie Drishyam in which the protagonist, Vijay Salgaokar played by Ajay Devgan who is charged with the murder of a teenage boy who went missing on 2nd Oct in rural Goa, where Vijay Salgaokar stays with his family. He visits Panjim on 3rd Oct and makes it a point to have memorable interactions with the bus conductor, the movie projectionist and the hotel owner. He visits Panjim again with his family and meets the same set of people and very tactfully uses hand gestures in linking their first interaction with a set of dates, i.e. 2nd & 3rd Oct, the dates when the boy went missing. Thereby preparing them as eyewitnesses, who would later go on to vouch for them in front of the police officers, that he & his family had actually traveled to Panjim on 2nd and 3rd Oct, stating their testimony as witness with 100% belief. This would make it impossible for the police to prove that he or his family had committed the crime."

"In this case I identified the key goal to get maximum traction. Understood the venue layout and chose,  the stall at the entrance of the dining hall by matching the pattern of the placement of credit card sales kiosks and got a screen to display a catchy presentation explaining the company's platform."

"Good. This was quick and focussed," said Chanakya.

Chanakya continued, "Now that we have a fair understanding of your personality and strengths. Let's summarize it before moving to the next step."

Tushar replied, "Sure."

Tushar pulled out a diary from his bag and started summarizing. He wrote,

**Source of energy:** Internal, Nature: Introverted

**Information processing:** Intuitive, connecting the dots type.

**Decision-making mechanism:** Feeling based

**Approach:** Methodical.

## Strengths:

1. Ability to abstract key drivers of a given situation.

2. Pattern recognition to match situations from memory.

3. Pattern recognition to come up with solutions from memory.

Tushar passed the diary to Chanakya to review. Taking a deep breath, he said, "I feel like I have super-powers that I myself wasn't consciously aware of. It feels good to jot them down and be able to read them."

Chanakya with a beaming smile took the dairy from Tushar and said, "One need not be a superhero to have superpowers, every person has some superpower or the other, the task is to find it, hone it and put it for your own and others good to create value."

Chanakya then looked and said, "This looks condensed. Let's now understand your aspiration and motivation."

# Chapter 3

# The Why of the Aspiration

Chanakya took a deep breath, looked at Tushar intently, and then asked, "What is your aspiration in life?"[7]

Tushar was caught off guard and said rhetorically, "To make a lot of money."

Chanakya smiled and said, "Money is a means, it can't be the end. Think again and answer."

Tushar took a pause and said, "I dream of living a common man's life. Get promoted timely, get married, have kids, get them a good education, have my own home & vehicle, get my kids married timely, retire early and pursue my passion post retirement."

---

7. Reference: This chapter is inspired from the book Primed to Perform: How to Build the Highest Performing Cultures Through the Science of Total Motivation by Lindsay McGregor and Neel Doshi

Chanakya smiled again and said, "This is nice, but why wait to pursue your passion till retirement, when all the other things can be done timely, why not pursue your passion timely too?"

"Come on, such things only happen in fairy tales or to a few lucky individuals," said Tushar in a sarcastic tone.

Chanakya asked, "Don't you consider yourself lucky?"

"Really? let's be practical, you know what I mean," said Tushar in a frustrated tone.

"Practicality is good till it forbids you from doing what is best for you not just now, but in the long run," said Chanakya in a calming voice.

Chanakya continued, "By accepting your current situation as your final destination, is nothing but giving up on your dreams. Yes, you do need to accept the current situation in its entirety of where you are today. But this does not mean that you give up on your final destination or your dream. Only when you can understand the distinction between the two and hold your dream without losing hope, will you be able to figure out strategies to transition from your current situation to your final destination."

Tushar looked like he had a eureka moment. He thought to himself, had he given up on his dream in the day-to-day hustle of today? It was hard for him to accept, but to be honest he had. He tried to hide his disgust and said, "Isn't that what most people do?"

Chanakya smiled and said yes, "They do. But, do you want to be like most people?"

Tushar meekly said, "No. But how can I have a different outcome where everyone is finding their current situation to be difficult?"

"By making different choices," responded Chanakya in a resounding voice.

Tushar said, "Okay. It sounds nice, but can you explain to me how?"

Chanakya started, "Our lives are an outcome of our circumstances. When we do not exercise the power of free will nature has bestowed upon us by making choices, we accept the default and live like zombies. This ranges from accepting the default settings like the ones on your phone and living by accepted social beliefs."

Tushar got a vague idea. But needed more relatable instances. The look on his face conveyed the same.

Chanakya took a pause and began. "Okay, let me explain with examples. Do you find all the notifications that pop up on your phone important?"

"No. Most of them are a distraction", replied Tushar.

"What do you do about it?" inquired Chanakya.

"Well, I turn my phone to silent to avoid them," replied Tushar.

"In the process, do you miss important calls or messages or other notifications?" asked Chanakya.

"Sometimes," replied Tushar.

"Are you aware that you can change the notification settings?", asked Chanakya.

"Yes, but that requires effort and thinking, and I have other important things to do," said Tushar.

"Exactly, it requires thinking consciously and making a decision. Which has a cognitive effort attached. But the beauty is, it is a one time effort. Once you do it, you have customized your phone to your personal preference. Isn't it worth to invest that one time effort for long-term benefits?", Chanakya questioned.

"Now that I think of it from a renewed perspective, yes." Tushar accepted.

"Similarly, don't you choose your course, job, or stream based on pre-defined preferences?" asked Chanakya.

Tushar took a pause and said, "Maybe now that I know I shall do it with my phone. But could you shed some more light to help me understand how?"

"Sure. Did you thoroughly analyze the streams for your graduation, or was that decision influenced by what others said? Did you pick your job based on matching long-term aspirations or you picked the one that paid the highest package, a commonly accepted decision method?" enquired Chanakya.

Tushar took a sip of water from the bottle near him and said, "Yes". But defended himself again by saying, "I guess that is what everyone does."

"Not everyone, but yes, most do. But like we discussed, you want to have different outcomes than everyone and for that, you will need to do things differently than how everyone else does!" exclaimed Chanakya.

Tushar became quiet and started thinking from the renewed perspective he had just discovered. He could see what Chanakya was explaining. He couldn't believe he had made so many decisions without thinking consciously, based on what the established social norm was. He started feeling sick about himself and began to get into a self blaming spiral. His expression gave a glimpse of what he was going through.

Chankya sensed Tushar's emotional state and said, "I can understand what you are going through. This realization can make one feel like they have been living life till now without much conscious thought. Sorry about that. But please understand the point of making you realize this is to enable you and help you understand dispassionately where you currently stand. Post this once you decide, you can be where you want to be. This understanding of your current location will help you strategize and act on how you make the transition to your desired position."

Chanakya's words got Tushar back to his senses. He began to think rationally again and regained his composure. He sipped a few sips of water and looked at Chanakya, as if he was trying to say, let's continue!

Chanakya continued, "So let me ask you in another way, what are the shows and movies you have enjoyed watching?"

Tushar started, "I have always enjoyed watching shows like the good old, DuckTales, TailSpin, Jungle Book movies like Sarfarosh, Drishyam, Talvar and The Shawshank Redemption."[8]

"Okay, why did you enjoy them? Can you identify a common theme?", asked Chanakya.

"I found the central character inspiring or the plot to be interesting. For instance, the thrill, courage & strategy with which Uncle Scrooge overcame situations in DuckTales,[9] the tact with which Baloo maneuvered his opponents,[10] how the CBI Inspector identified Gulfam Hasan to be the kingpin in the supply of illegal arms in Sarfarosh,[11] how Vijay outsmarted the investigation team to protect his family in Drishyam,[12] how the CBI officer figured out the real criminals despite the tampered evidence of the murder case in Talvar[13] and how Andy Dufresne got the better of the warden to become a freeman again in The Shawshank Redemption."[14] replied Tushar.

---

8. Reference: Drishyam (2015) hindi movie.

9. Reference: DuckTales (TV Series 1987–1990)

10. Reference: TaleSpin (TV Series 1990–1991)

11. Reference: Sarfarosh (1999) hindi movie.

12. Reference: Drishyam (2015) hindi movie.

13. Reference: Talvar (2015) hindi movie.

14. Reference: The Shawshank Redemption (1994), english movie.

Tushar paused and then continued. "Now that I think of it, I liked their personalities. The fact that they were so good at what they did. It was as if they possessed a natural talent for the situation they had at hand. They were able to comprehend a situation, recognize the pattern, pick a solution, sort of mentally simulate the solution and execute it to perfection by improvising."

"That's an insightful analysis indeed! So, you saw yourself in them & them in yourself?" asked Chanakya.

Tushar was taken aback. It astonished him at how his choices resonated with his personality and his strengths.

He said, "Yes, I have never had this perspective before. Now it all makes sense to me. I feel so much better with just this realization."

"I am glad you do. Now tell me, what kind of games do you like to play?", Chanakya asked.

"Well, I like cricket, chess, bridge, treasure hunts & solving mysteries." replied Tushar.

"Okay. You have mentioned cricket before, too. What were you good at in cricket apart from bowling?" asked Chanakya.

"Apart from bowling, my key contribution towards the team's success was to read the opposition well and strategize our game. I was good at finding weaknesses through my observations and the ability to recognize patterns. With my bowling & analytical skills, I would often take early wickets and play a critical role in my team's success. My teammates valued my advice owing to its effectiveness." said Tushar.

"That makes sense. Why did you like the other games?", asked Chanakya.

"Chess & bridge are games where you need skill along with luck. Treasure hunts & solving mysteries. I love them because they give me a platform to be rewarded for my strategic and analytical skills." replied Tushar.

He further added, "I have always enjoyed playing treasure hunts to uncover mysteries, be it as a kid or later in college. I like using my analytical thinking to solve such situations. It gives me immense thrill and satisfaction. In real life, I enjoy helping people see what others can't. It quenches my thirst for feeling special. If my profession offered me this kind of fulfillment, I would never take a day off & work on weekends, too".

"Wow! That's quite a statement! I think we have enough to move to the next step." said Chanakya.

Chanakya continued, "Now tell me, why do you like what you like? Be it watching a show or a movie? Or playing a game?"

"Because it is fun!" Tushar replied immediately.

"Okay. What makes it fun?" Chanakya probed.

"Because it does not feel like homework or assignment, lol!", said Tushar.

Chanakya said, "Exactly!"

"How do you feel then?" Chanakya prodded further.

"It feels effortless, like I have an avenue to visualize it and express myself" responded Tushar.

"Do you ever get tired of these?" asked Chanakya.

"Never!" replied Tushar.

"Do you experience a state of play?" asked Chanakya.

"Yes, like I said, I do it because it is effortless to me. I just flow seamlessly. There comes a time where I get so engrossed doing this that I forget my own existence." replied Tushar.

"Okay. That's comprehensive. Now tell me, Why did you like Jungle Book? Tell me if there is another reason apart from the one you shared." asked Chanakya.

"Well. I love animals! I feel they love unconditionally." replied Tushar.

"Yes, they do." said Chanakya.

Chanakya continued, "Do you have any goals of having pets or doing something for animal welfare?"

"Yes. I want to have pets. In fact I want to open animal shelters for stray animals." replied Tushar with a beaming smile.

"That's a noble idea! You must do so." said Chanakya.

"Does your doing so depend on whether you are paid for it?" inquired Chanakya.

"Of Course not! In fact I would do it with my own money. It's something that's close to my heart. It's one of my life's purposes." replied Tushar immediately.

"Great! So that's one of your purposes in life." said Chanakya.

"Now tell me, why are we having this discussion?" asked Chanakya.

"To figure out ways to improve my future and to get into a career that is fulfilling for me." replied Tushar.

"Right. Can we call it Potential?" asked Chanakya.

"Sure. But I don't understand why you are asking all this, when we have got the basic idea I guess." replied Tushar.

"Patience Tushar." said Chanakya.

He continued, "Do you remember the movie 3 idiots? Do you remember when Farhan goes to his father on the day of the interview to allow him to pursue wildlife photography?"

"Yes, I do distinctly", says Tushar.

"Do you remember one line his father says, that is typically used by Indian parents?" asked Chanakya.

"Are you referring to what Mr. Kapoor would think?", asked Tushar.

"Yes. What would you call that kind of tactic?", asked Chanakya.

"Emotional blackmail." said Tushar smilingly.

"Can we get the emotion out and call it emotional pressure?" said Chanakya with a wink.

"Okay, as you say." replied Tushar.

"Have you seen people do jobs they don't like for monetary obligations?" asked Chanakya.

"Yes, people have fixed expenses like monthly installments, living expenses, rent, school fee, etc. That they have to pay on a monthly basis. If their monthly salary does not come by the end of the month, they would have a tough time managing their budget and drawing into their savings. This thought itself is scary and hence people tolerate the job that they don't like to keep their monthly cash inflow intact." said Tushar.

"That's comprehensive! Let's call this economic pressure." said Chanakya.

Chanakya continued, "Do you know when people do day-to-day activities without thinking, as if they were a zombie?"

"I don't think many would be doing this. But let me be honest. I am guilty of it. This has happened to me before in school & college life, too. Once something becomes monotonous, I end up doing it without asking, on an autopilot." said Tushar.

Chanakya smiled and said, "it happens to all of us. We have all been guilty of it at some point in time or the other. Also do you think this is limited to an activity or can it happen in a job too?"

"I am not sure about others. But for sure it is happening with me in my job." said Tushar.

"I appreciate your honesty. It can happen to anyone in a job, Tushar." said Chanakya.

He continued, "Can we call it inertia?"

"Inertia, at rest, in motion or of direction", asked Tushar cheekily.

"That's interesting! Why don't you tell me?" Chanakya immediately asked.

"Well, that was pun-intended." said Tushar.

"Ha Ha. I understand, Tushar. But it seems like your pun intended statement can help you gain an invaluable insight." said Chanakya with a wink.

"Okay. I am confused between Inertia, in **motion and of direction**. I kind of know it is inertia of motion. Since we are talking about day-to-day work. But then what is inertia of direction?" asked a curious Tushar.

Chankaya said, "Right again. Hold on to that question. It's one of paramount importance. We will address it in a while."

Chanakya continued, "Now tell me, what do you think the part we discussed from play to inertia are?"

Tushar thought for a while. He looked confused. He said, "I think the Play, Purpose & Potential seem to be good reasons for doing something, w/hile Economic pressure, Emotional pressure & Inertia seem to be drag-like reasons for doing something. So I think they are sort of reasons to do a particular thing like a workpiece or a job. Do you think my understanding is correct?"

"Yes, it is. You got it right. Like you said, they are like the reasons for doing something. Another word for it would be motivation. It is the WHY of doing something." said Chanakya.

Tushar had a eureka moment when he heard the word motivation. It all made sense to him now. In that moment he knew why he could continue bowling at the top of his game when he was tired or why he could continue searching for cues in a treasure hunt when he was gasping to even breathe properly. He also understood why he felt out of place in his current role.

With an enormous sigh of relief, Tushar said, "Thank you!"

"You are most welcome! Now to make sure you retain what we discussed, can you summarize it?" asked Chanakya.

Tushar without saying anything started writing,

Motivation is why we do something. There are two kinds of motivations:

A. Good

Following are the good motivations:

1.  **Play:** The state of flow. When you do something because you enjoy doing it. Like I enjoy bowling or playing treasure hunt.

2.  **Purpose:** You do something as you consider it to serve a higher purpose you believe in. Like Animal welfare.

3.  **Potential:** You do something as you consider the current activity would help you achieve something bigger in life. Like my conversation with Chanakya for a better career.

B. Drag

Following are the drag motivations:

1.  **Emotional pressure:** When one does something as they are feeling socially pressurized to do it. Like Farhan's father's dialogue in the movie 3 Idiots, What would Mr. Kapoor say? when Farhan asked his dad for permission to pursue photography instead of engineering as a career.

2.  **Economic pressure:** When one does something as they need the money that is paid for the job to run their expenses, family, etc. Like an artist doing accounting work to run his family.

3.  **Inertia:** One keeps doing something repetitively without knowing why they are doing it. Like me doing my job.

He then gave what he had written to Chanakya.

Chanakya glanced through it and said, "That is well summarized. But I want you to be easy on yourself and not judge yourself too hard. Can you do that for me?"

Tushar nodded. He then said, "Now that I know where I stand, can we now move to the solution?"

Chanakya smiled and said, "We will after discussing a few more important things. You have understood yourself to a degree, but not enough yet, to come to the solution. So hold your horses."

Chanakya continued, "The first 3 motivations that you have listed under good are in ascending order and the last 3 are in descending order."

Tushar asked in a confused manner, "Could you explain that please?"

"Sure. On the good side of motivation, Play is a better motivation than purpose, and purpose is better than potential. On the drag side of motivation, inertia is the worst, economic pressure is better than inertia and emotional pressure is better than economic pressure. To bridge the good and drag motivations into a holistic spectrum, potential is better motivation than emotional pressure." Chanakya replied.

"That makes sense. Thank you!", said Tushar.

"Now that you know the motivation spectrum, you can map a work to your internal motivation and make conscious choices. This is not to say that you should always do work only that is connected to good motivations, but in the long-run you must gravitate towards good motivation oriented work, to make the most of your true potential." said Chanakya.

"Okay. Now with this in mind. Tell me, what did you aspire to become as a kid? Before you answer this, think of something that actually appealed to the core of your being and not something you liked on the surface." asked Chanakya.

Tushar took a pause and started thinking.

The coffee vendor came at the right time. Both of them had the urge to refresh themselves. It was around 6.30 pm. Both ordered a strong coffee.

Tushar kept thinking while taking sips of warm coffee in between. While Chanakya took a break and enjoyed his coffee.

Chanakya, through his questions, had helped Tushar get a grip of where he stood and see hope at the same time. He made him see a direct connection between his choices and his personality & strengths. Tushar could see that people appreciated him for who he was and for his top skills. This made him relax and gave him the mind space to think in a stress-free manner. Then Chanakya made him understand the motivation spectrum and his motivation for various activities that he enjoyed, like bowling, treasure hunt, etc. While also helping him realize that inertia had been his primary motivation in his current role.

Fifteen minutes later, once both of them had finished their coffee and felt refreshed,

Tushar started, "**I have always wanted to be a strategist. I enjoy strategizing and seeing my strategy take roots and grow in the real world. One of my neighbors was an MBA in finance and worked for a local milk cooperative. He would have a chat with me whenever I went to his house. He used to check about my studies and things in general. I was kind of open with him. I would often enquire about his work. He would narrate fascinating stories on how he was involved in planning the collection of milk from new areas, setting up new factories and resolving business problems. My aspiration resonated with him the most. Hence, I chose to pursue an MBA in finance.**"

Chanakya took a pause and then spoke. "I see. Do you remember your neighbor's job designation?"

"No, I am not in contact with him anymore. As their family shifted. I have tried looking for him, but haven't been able to locate him." responded Tushar.

"I understand. No problem. We can do the extrapolation of his role based on our understanding and then take things from there." Said Chanakya.

He continued, "By your account of his job responsibilities. He would have been in a strategic role in the field of corporate finance or corporate strategy. Does that make sense to you?"

"Yes, it does. In fact, I tried a lot in my placement days to get into roles related to corporate finance, corporate strategy & management consulting. The sad part was none of the companies that offered campus placements had this role and the ones that were available off campus, demanded education from a top rated MBA Institute. I had to compromise and take the best campus placements offered to me. I hoped to have some bit of strategy, at least in this role, but then reality hit me." replied Tushar with a dejected smile.

Chanakya said, "You must accept the present moment graciously. Only then can you move towards what you truly want and deserve. How many times are you going to be sad about the same thing? Does that help in any way?"

"Play the cards you have been dealt as if you wanted them." He added.

Tushar understood the crux of Chanakya's communication. He gathered & composed himself. Then said, "Okay, let's move on!"

Chanakya said, "That's the spirit! So, your aspiration is to get into strategic roles. Where you can use your abstraction, pattern recognition, and mental simulation strengths to create value, right?"

Tushar smiled and said, "Yes. Thanks for connecting my strengths to my aspiration and enabling me to see hope. My dejected state of mind can make my thinking clouded. I feel better now. Thank you!"

"You are most welcome", said Chanakya.

# Chapter 4

# Transforming Beliefs - From Foe to Ally.

The time was 7 pm and the super fast train was cruising at peak pace. All the lights in the compartment were lit and almost everyone was awake. People were engaged in a variety of conversations. One could overhear discussions about politics, recent events, bollywood, etc. But Tushar, with unwavering focus, was completely pulled into the self-discovery conversation he was having with Chanakya. He wondered why he had not put efforts in understanding himself, his motivation for everything that he did and his aspirations. He thought to himself, yes I had not carried out such an extensive and insightful exercise that I just did. But I had an intuitive idea about who I am, why I do a certain thing and what I want to do. It wasn't as clear as it is now, but it was clear enough for him to serve as an effective compass to guide him. Ideally, it should have guided him, but it didn't. Without any further thought, he asked Chanakya the same question.

As soon as Chanakya heard the question, he smiled coyly and said, "Good that you asked this question. Logically, understanding this before discussing the solution is very important. It will help you dissect the problem and reach to its core, and you can only solve any problem completely once you have understood its root cause."

Chanakya continued, "Why don't you attempt to answer this? When you had a vague idea about your preferences, why did you make different choices?"

Tushar started thinking. It seemed counterintuitive to have known his preferences and made choices that were different, sometimes opposite.

He checked with Chanakya, "The social pressure?"

Chanakya replied, "Sort of. But that's just the surface level cause. What do you think it produces?"

Tushar thought for a minute and asked, "assumptions?"

"Okay, what type of assumptions?" cross questioned Chanakya.

"Assumptions about what you can do and what you cannot do?" replied Tushar.

"Okay, how has it made you make different choices from what is best for you?" asked Chanakya.

"It led me to choose science for class 11th as the long held social belief is, bright students take science. Then it led me to choose and pursue engineering, as society considered it a good choice for students who take mathematics. Commonly held social beliefs also led me to choose Information Technology (IT), as my engineering stream, as India had become an IT hub and IT professionals were drawing the fattest paychecks. I did an MBA immediately after my engineering due to the same reason, with little thought. As a lot of people told me, focussing on studies becomes difficult after a few years of job experience and hence it's wise to finish your MBA just after your engineering. The choice of my college too was influenced by commonly held beliefs for both my engineering and MBA, which were based on some well accepted ranking. Accepting the job offer too was influenced by the same, based on who paid the highest salary.", said Tushar.

"Comprehensive. You seem to have understood it well." said Chanakya.

He continued, "Did all the above choices turn out to be good for you?"

"Some of them did. Most did not. I think I would have made different choices had I thought about what was best for me." said Tushar.

"Okay, fair enough. Can you help me identify the sources of these social beliefs, assumptions, or biases?" asked Chanakya.

Tushar took a moment and started, "opinions of family members, relatives, teachers & friends?"

"Yes, they are definitely there. But what about the other subtle forms in which opinions or assumptions seep into your head?" asked Chanakya.

"Do you mean movies & books we watch & read?" cross questioned Tushar.

"Yes, that's there, too. What about news channels, newspapers, magazines & idolizing someone?" asked Chanakya.

Tushar took a pause and replied," you are right, I never thought of it this way."

"Good. Happy realization!" said Chanakya.

He continued, "In fact any form of communication has two components: data or facts and opinion."

Tushar was a bit confused. He requested Chanakya to elaborate.

Chanakya continued, "When we say something, we are trying to draw an inference or meaning from a fact or data. This inference is an opinion. The type of opinion we draw depends a great deal on our beliefs & assumptions. For example, one person looks at the first rain and says, today I will enjoy hot snacks with tea in the evening. Another person says, hell I will have to walk today in the muddy streets. In both the cases rain is the fact. However, enjoying hot snacks with tea or worrying about walking in muddy streets are opinions that are coloured by our assumptions and beliefs. We formed the assumptions and beliefs over time through our experiences. Experiences can be either direct or indirect. In this context we will dig deeper into indirect experiences. These hinge on other people's experiences. They can come from a person, book, movie, news, or any other media. As such experiences get repeated and/or pronounced, they make the belief or assumption stronger."

Tushar now got a hang of it. He said, "but can we overcome it? If yes, how?"

Chanakya smiled and answered, "Yes we can, with consciousness. Since beliefs and assumptions are deep-rooted in our psychology, they form a part of our subconscious mind. Which means we are not even aware how they influence our thinking, unless we make a conscious effort to overcome the same."

Tushar said, "Okay. Now I get it. Is this why so many spiritual preachers talk so much about the term consciousness? That's a rhetorical question, of course they do. No wonder! It is so very important in our lives. But why don't educated people apply it?"

You are right. "In fact, It is the most important thing in life. Consciousness is what separates you from any other living being. Most people do not realize the importance of it or pretend to understand it, however their understanding is pretty shallow. Hence they never are able to apply it. Consciousness, in essence, is the ability to make choices by deliberately considering the impact of each action and choosing an action while being completely aware of its consequences and accepting 100% responsibility for the same."

"This makes perfect sense to me. Thank you!", said Tushar.

"Another thing, while education is a good, nice thing. It is highly overrated. It is a good complement to have, but it is far from being the only qualification." said Chanakya.

"I intuitively agree with you on education being overrated. But what is the key complement to education?" asked Tushar

"Skill. It is the ability to apply what you know as knowledge. If knowledge is potential energy, skill is kinetic energy." said Chanakya.

"Wow! That's insightful!", said Tushar.

He continued, "But then why do employers give so much weightage to education & years of experience?"

"What would you do if you were the employer?" Chanakya cross questioned this time.

Tushar thought for a minute and said, I would look for proxies for skill.

Chanakya smiled and asked again, "and what would that proxy be?"

Tushar said, "Experience & Education."

See, "You are looking at the same parameters that a typical employer looks at." said Chanakya.

"Yes, but I would see the two differently." resisted Tushar.

"Fair enough. Can you elaborate?" asked Chanakya.

Sure, "I would look for the application of education in terms of projects and internships and the quality of experience, by that I mean look at the grasping power of the individual." explained Tushar.

"Okay, that seems like the right way to do things." Said Chanakya.

"Then why do employers make the interviewing process an interrogation process instead of keeping it a discovery process?" asked a frustrated Tushar.

"Well, that's an insight!" exclaimed Chanakya.

He continued, "Tell me what would you do if you had to fill a role in quick turnaround time & had hundreds of resumes to go through? Would you be able to follow the discovery process for each candidate?" asked Chanakya.

"I would have to filter the resumes and shortlist candidates based on proxies that can be checked on paper like education and experience mentioned in the resume." replied Tushar.

Tushar was taken aback. He realized that the timeline to fill a role and the volume of candidates was the key cause that led employers to filter candidates based on education and experience mentioned in the resume.

He then asked, "Is this need for a shortcut the reason for building brands in education and prestigious past employers?"

"True and the social approval reinforces it." replied Chanakya.

"Now I understand why it is tough to get an interview call in the first place without a gold standard education or past experience. The interview stage is fairly explorative & discovery oriented, but there is still scope for significant improvement." spoke Tushar, thinking out aloud.

"Indeed. It is the part about getting a seat at the table, which is difficult. The rest is better, but is not optimum, yet on an average." agreed Chanakya.

"Now that we have understood that getting a seat at the table is the difficult part, how do I overcome it?" asked an impatient Tushar.

"Bypass the process, reinvent it." replied Chanakya immediately.

"Okay. But how?" asked a confused Tushar.

"Avoid the intermediaries and approach the key decision maker." responded Chanakya.

"And will he listen to me?" asked Tushar.

"Well, if you speak in a language he understands, he will." replied Chanakya.

"Come on! Please tell me, how?" asked an irritated Tushar.

"I meant it. By speaking a language, he would understand. Let me explain. Showcase the outcomes of your work. That will help them see the linkage between your skill and application." replied Chanakya.

"Okay. Now I understand. But how will I find an opportunity to do that?" asked Tushar.

"You will need to improvise depending on the situation. Do you see how you would be choosing differently by following this approach?" asked Chanakya.

"Yes, I do." Said Tushar.

He took a pause, as if allowing himself to absorb everything. He had understood the root cause of why people end up choosing a career that is not best suited for them. Why employers value education and years of work experience in their filtration process and how that benefits brand reinforcement of prestigious educational institutes and past employers.

But he couldn't understand that once people become aware of their ill-suited choices, why didn't they change to align themselves to their aspirations & strengths? He kept thinking, but was still unable to wrap his head around it. So, he finally put it up to Chanakya as a question.

"That's a good question!" exclaimed Chanakya.

He continued, "What do you think the reason is Tushar?"

Tushar thought for a while and said, "Maybe monotony sets in and they too are afraid of change."

Chanakya said, "That definitely happens, but something more tangible happens before that, again led by preset beliefs and assumptions about how to lead a successful life."

He continued, "As people age, their responsibilities increase and they use borrowings to purchase pseudo assets that get them special approval and enhance their status."

"You mean borrowing for day-to-day expenses and living beyond their means?" asked Tushar.

"Borrowing for day-to-day expenses is a bit extreme. Some people do go that far on the dopamine of borrowed funds, but there are other ways to live beyond one's means. This includes lifestyle habits that are costly, it also includes borrowing early in their career to buy a house or a car, etc." added Chanakya.

"Buying a house and a car are necessities!" exclaimed Tushar.

"Are they? Do you own a house or a car of your own?" asked Chanakya.

"No, I don't." replied Tushar.

"Does that make your life miserable?" asked Chanakya.

"No, it doesn't. But everyone wants to buy a house to have a sense of security and a car for comfortable travel after a point in time." replied Tushar.

"The key point to be noted, my lord, is after a point in time. Let's consider the house for now, as it is a significantly larger purchase. Can you tell me how late can one purchase their house without risking too much?" asked Chanakya.

"Mid-way through their career, I guess." replied Tushar.

Okay. "An average career spans 35 years from the age of 25 to 60. That puts this purchase at the age of 42 years. Do you think people today wait till 42 to buy their house?" probed Chanakya.

"No, they don't. They buy it mostly within the first 5-7 years of starting their career." replied Tushar.

"Okay. Why do you think people do that?" asked Chanakya.

"Ofcourse, to make the best use of their surplus funds." replied Tushar.

"Are you sure?" asked Chanakya.

"Ofcourse. They buy security and peace by buying their own house." responded Tushar.

"Do they buy security or sell themselves into slavery by buying a house early in life?" inquired Chanakya.

"What? I don't understand how?" asked a confused Tushar.

"Okay. Early in life most people start off with a salary that leaves them little surplus, if at all they are into savings. As the years pass, their salary grows and so does their surplus. Would you agree to that?" asked Chanakya.

"Yes", said Tushar.

Chanakya continued, "Okay do you know the property price to individual income ratio in Delhi?"

"No", replied Tushar.

"It is around 16.5 times. Which means assuming the average current annual income to be constant, it would take the average decent earning person 16.5 years worth of salary to buy the house." explained Chanakya.

"Oh that's a lot!" Exclaimed a shocked Tushar.

"It is. It turns out the average EMI to salary ratio is 37%, which means for an average person earning, say, Rs. 1 Lakh per month, Rs. 37,000 goes towards payment of the EMI for the house." said Chanakya.

Hell, that's a lot! exclaimed Tushar.

"If you as a single person with little responsibilities feel that way, imagine the situation for a single earning member who has the responsibility of his whole family on him." said Chanakya.

"I get your point now. It's a drain on the monthly budget, but how does it enslave people?" asked Tushar.

"EMI is an expense that one can't avoid. One has to pay for it. Since it's a significant portion of salary, it is dependent on the salary. You are dependent on your employer for your salary. Yes you can always get another job, but can you change from one track that you choose because it paid you well in the first place to one that you are passionate about with the same salary?" asked Chanakya.

"Only if they are close, that too requires a lot of variables like an open-minded employer, demand for the role etc. Usually the talent acquisition folks label you and it's very difficult." said a dejected Tushar.

"Yes. But it's not the talent acquisition folks who are at fault completely. It's the system that presses them against humongous volumes of candidates and allows them little time." said Chanakya.

He continued, "This leads people to stay in the same or similar roles, even if they change employers. The shackles of EMI leaves them at the beck and call of their employer and in a role that sucks the life out of them as it's not aligned to their aspirations and strengths. Overtime monotony sets in and they turn into living zombies. Now add a car loan, a personal loan and credit card loan to that and think of that person's state of mind."

"That would be colossal. No wonder my father always advised me to stay away from borrowings." said Tushar.

"Borrowing per se is not bad. But if used to acquire liabilities that are labeled as assets by the society and/or for meeting living expenses can turn into a vicious borrowing trap.

You can always purchase a house on a loan at a later point in time like you said mid-career. By then you would have saved a decent amount & if you invest it well it could be significant too. This would enable you to have psychological freedom and allow you to make choices aligned to your aspiration and strengths." said Chanakya.

"And what did you mean by expensive lifestyle habits? Did you mean gambling?" asked a curious Tushar.

"Ha ha. Gambling is an extreme again. What I meant was buying expensive phones, watches, laptops, shoes, clothing etc. In fact anything branded just to show off and gain social status without any consideration for the real benefits. It's something that people don't realize early-on as the ramifications of such a habit is seen in the long run." said Chanakya.

He continued, "If you see all these, be it buying a house or car early in life or buying expensive & branded stuff gets one social status? It is a default path that society considers as a proxy for people who are successful. So much so that the choice of a partner is based quite often on such proxies. Everyone wants to be successful, if not at least appear successful. This leads them to a path that takes them away from their passion."

"It's shocking how much influence our environment has on our thinking. I never ever realized this. Thank you so much!" said an enlightened & grateful Tushar.

He continued, "Between, if not invest in houses, cars and other tangible stuff. Where does one invest?"

Chanakya smiled and said, "You can invest in stocks & businesses in the initial part of your career to build wealth.

By doing so you would get compounding, the 8th wonder in the world work for you!"

"You seem to know investing. Can you teach me?" asked a curious Tushar.

"Sure. But that is a topic for another day. Right now I am famished and tired. Let's have dinner and sleep." said Chanakya.

Both had their dinner and went to bed.

# Chapter 5

# Career Landscape

Tushar woke up with a jolt. He rubbed his eyes and looked at his watch, it was 7 am in the morning. He saw a tea vendor passing his seat. He asked, "Which station is it?"

"Pendra Road", the vendor responded.

"Okay. Never heard of it before. Which state are we in?" asked Tushar.

"We have just entered Chhattisgarh", responded the vendor and walked forward.

Tushar got down from his seat. He looked around and could not find Chanakya at his seat. He headed to the washroom to freshen up. When he returned, Chanakya was waiting for him, with freshly made puri sabzi and tea for both of them. Chanakya asked Tushar to have a seat and they enjoyed the freshly made puri sabzi. After finishing breakfast, while sipping his tea, Chanakya said, Today we will be discussing the most important part of our career planning.

Tushar got excited. He hurriedly asked, "Are you going to tell me which career options are best suited for me?"

"No. I am going to lay out a framework that empowers you to do it for yourself." replied Chanakya.

Tushar had not expected this type of an answer. He contemplated for a moment and spoke, "Sounds like you have quite a lot of insights in store for me this morning".

"This framework is going to have some really insightful ideas, but I assure you, the ideas will be easy to comprehend and assimilate." said Chanakya.

"Fair enough. Let's get going then." said Tushar.

"Sure. Do you think some jobs are better than others?" asked Chanakya.

"Yes. The ones that you get after placement from the so-called premier institutes. They offer a much better pay." said Tushar.

"Ah, pay. For the time being let us keep pay out of the equation. We will come to pay too, but let's look at other operational aspects first." said Chanakya.

He continued, "Now tell me apart from pay, do you think some jobs are better than others? If yes, why?"

"Yes, for sure. Some are way better than others." Tushar snapped.

He continued, "some jobs are better because they offer interesting work and other benefits which I think I know intuitively but I am unable to put them into words."

Chanakya said, "I understand. We will explore. Interesting work is definitely a key personal preference, we are right now going to focus on the key dimensions that define a job in a common framework. We will come to that later when we customize a job for you."

# 1. Impact:

Chanakya asked, "Do you think some roles have a higher impact than others?"

"Yes. That increases as you go higher up in the hierarchy." said Tushar.

"That's true. A manager who is responsible for managing multiple individuals definitely has a larger impact. What my question meant was, considering two people at the same level, do you think some roles have a larger impact than others?" asked Chanakya.

Tushar started to think. He took a longer than usual pause and said, I guess the closer someone is to the sales function the larger the impact he has.

"Are you sure about that?" asked Chanakya immediately.

"I think so." replied Tushar.

"Well in that case Sales as a team should have the largest impact. isn't it?" asked Chanakya.

"Yes, more sales folks can sell more products and drive higher sales. right?" Tushar cross questioned.

"True. Having more people to sell is always a great thing as it helps in generating more sales, but what happens when the product/service itself is not good enough? In such a case more sales force would increase the cost without contributing higher sales, thereby eroding the profitability or causing a loss." said Chanakya.

He continued, "What do you think now, is it closeness to sales or the relative importance of the role in the company's value chain?"

"I am not sure. But I think it is the relative importance of the role in the company's value chain. Is that correct?" asked a confused Tushar.

"Yes, that is correct. Let me explain. Before sales, it's important to develop the right product/service. A great sales team without a great product/service is similar to a person with a loud mouth that promises a lot, but delivers little due to lack of any substantial content. Once you have a great product/service, the next most important thing is to be able to communicate it to your customers well. Also, for a company to run smoothly, the company needs to have a high performing & inclusive culture that bonds different functions into a unified force and enables the achievement of business goals." explained Chanakya.

"Yes, that makes sense. I get the gist of it. Can you help me understand with a few more concrete examples?" asked Tushar.

Chanakya continued, "Sure. Let's first take the example of an IT based product company. To build a great product, you need a good product development team that works in a disciplined manner. A product manager is a role that ensures understanding of the functioning of a product from a functional standpoint. Then they need to be able to convert it into technical requirement and pass it on to the engineering team that comprises of software developers to develop it, which then is tested by the quality assurance team against the functional description provided by the product manager. Can you see the amount of influence the product manager has in the whole product development to go live in the value chain?"

"Yes I do", said Tushar.

"Now let's invert and verify our findings. What would happen if the product manager misunderstood a function requirement?" asked Chanakya.

"It would lead to wrong technical requirements being passed on, based on which the developers would develop a feature and the quality assurance would pass it based on the flawed functional description by the product manager and a not required feature would go live." said Tushar after doing a connective thinking out loud.

Chanakya said, "Yes. Do you think it would cost the business?"

"Ofcourse, dearly." replied Tushar.

"That verifies our finding that the product manager as a role is a really an important one. Do you think product managers involved in development or enhancement of features in any other industry other than IT would be important going by the same analogy?" asked Chanakya.

"Yes, that is a logical and obvious thing. In software product development a misunderstood financial understanding would cost majorly future salaries. If the business was car making or paint making, it would cost us the material and other costs too including future salaries." said Tushar.

"Good! You are a quick learner." complimented Chanakya.

He continued, "Let's look at a few more examples, but this time we will do it differently. I will ask you if a role is a high impact role or not and you can answer with an explanation supporting your answer. Are you ready, Tushar?"

"Raring to go!" Tushar responded with a beaming smile.

"What do you think about the role of a trainer? Is it a high impact role?" asked Chanakya.

"Of course. It is!" Tushar commented.

He continued, "The trainer is someone who is responsible for training multiple people in an organization and is in a strong position to create more impact through their influence."

"You are right." said Chanakya.

He continued, "What about an operations executive team member? Someone who is responsible to follow a process and is an individual contributor. Is it a high impact role?"

Tushar thought for a while and started, "I don't think so, as this person would be carrying out operations at an individual level and even if they do not perform well, it would not create a systemic impact."

"Interesting! You are right. Systemic impact is an effective term that you used to verify your conclusion." acknowledged Chanakya.

He continued, "How about a support engineer? Do you think it is a high impact role?"

"A support engineer gets to do a lot of firefighting. Occasionally based on how proactive that person is, they might identify a systemic issue and play a high impact role. But 95% of the time, they are involved in providing technical support to different individuals over call, chat or email. So I would say it is not a high impact role." remarked Tushar.

"That's comprehensive. Would that be true for customer care executives, relationship managers, and business development executives?" asked Chanakya.

"Yes, pretty much. They might look like high impact roles, but essentially they are dealing with clients one to one and not one to many." replied Tushar.

"One to one & not one to many, that's an insight! I agree with your understanding." said Chanakya.

"What about talent acquisition executives? They are involved in hiring, and hiring quality talent can create disproportionate impact for an organization. Is that a high impact role?" asked Tushar.

"Hiring quality talent definitely creates a disproportionate impact for an organization. But how often do these executives have the autonomy to decide? How often are they given time to scout for the right candidate? How are their incentives aligned?" asked Chanakya.

"Okay. Yes, they mostly follow directives by the hiring manager or a senior. They are pressed for time. Their incentives too are aligned to close roles as soon as possible." replied Tushar.

"Now you know why they are not a high impact role?" questioned Chanakya.

He continued, "How about an HR Executive? Do you think it is a high impact role?"

Tushar again began to think. After gathering his thoughts he started, "I am not sure about this one as I have two conflicting thoughts about the role as per my understanding. The work that they do behind the screens can sometimes be of high impact, but mostly it is more day to day operations in nature. However, owing to the nature of their role, the social connect they have and maintain with employees in the organization, especially in mid and small sized ones, it can be considered impactful. This is something I have heard from my friends who joined smaller organizations."

"Sounds like an interesting dilemma with a lot of conflicting thoughts! Let's dissect it and try to understand it better." said Chanakya.

He continued, "Your observation of the difference in importance of the role based on the size of the organization and hence social connections is correct. The idea behind asking you to label roles as high impact and non-high impact roles is to help you develop an understanding of the drivers that make a role. The high impact of a role varies from case to case and it completely depends on how much systemic impact a role has in the value chain. The larger is the systemic impact the more disproportionate is their impact and the vice-versa is also true."

"Now that you have a fair understanding of high impact roles and know that identifying one would need a thorough understanding of the role. Can you summarize how to identify a high impact role?" asked Chanakya.

"A role that has one to many impact through which they create disproportionate systemic impact would be a high impact role." replied Tushar.

"Sounds good. To solidify your learning. Can you share a few high impact roles and explain why each of them is a high impact role?" asked Chanakya.

"Sure," said Tushar.

He continued, **Following are the High Impact roles and their respective explanations:**

| Sl. No. | Role | Industry | Explanation |
| --- | --- | --- | --- |
| 1 | Database Administrator | IT | They manage the database that is often the backbone of IT companies. |
| 2 | Product Manager | IT & other Industries | They are involved in design & development of the functionality, aesthetics etc of a product. It could be an IT product, an online platform, an FMCG product, a vehicle etc. |
| 3 | Business Analyst | IT | They are either involved in product development/ project management and influence the product or process or both. |
| 4 | Buy-side Research Analyst | Investment Management | Unlike a sell-side research analyst who usually follows specified sectors and periodically looks at same companies with 1 quarter to 1 years time horizon.In the business of investment management, A buy-side research analyst actually searches for high return low risk opportunities to actually invest client's funds in. He is unlike a sell-side research analyst who usually follows specified sectors and periodically looks at the same companies with 1 quarter to 1 year time horizon. |

| | | | |
|---|---|---|---|
| 5 | Credit Analyst | Banks & NBFCs | Involved in evaluating the credit-worthiness of businesses they play a crucial role in approval of a loan and hence the asset quality of a bank or NBFC that they are working for. |
| 6 | Actuary | Insurance | They are involved in the crucial calculations that lead to the pricing of insurance contracts and exposure of insurance business to ensure diversification. |
| 7 | Learning & Development Executive | Across Industries | They are involved in propagating learning and development practices across the organisation. |
| 8 | Employee Engagement Executive | Across Industries | They are involved in developing a sense of bonding through various employee engagement activities in the organisation. |
| 9 | Organisational Development Executive | Acoss Industries | They are involved in efforts directed towards seamlessly developing the organisation internally. |
| 10 | UI/UX Designer/ Developer | IT & other Industries | They design the user interface or product or packaging, that is seen by potential customers and existing customers. |

| 11 | Content Writer/ Developer | Across Industries | These include specialized content writers/developers who develop key content that influences potential and& existing customers. |
|---|---|---|---|
| 12 | Marketing Executive | Across Industries | These would include marketing executives who are involved in drawing the marketing plan to make a product go viral in terms of popularity and sales. |

"That's learning condensed for a lifetime through real time application. Well done, Tushar!" exclaimed Chanakya.

# 2. Visibility:

"Sounds good, Now, let's look at the next dimension. Higher visibility." said Chanakya.

"Sure. That should be fairly straightforward. What is seen, sells." exclaimed Tushar.

"True. But in this, what is seen, Is it effort that is seen or the outcome?" asked Chanakya.

"Effort I guess." replied Tushar.

"Well, effort is important. But in business outcomes matter. So it's the outcome." Chanakya said.

"Can you help me understand the difference with an example?" requested Tushar.

"Sure. A trainer in a bank trains relentlessly and puts in a lot of effort in training sales people. His efforts are seen by many. But when his trainees perform well at their job is the outcome attributed to him?" asked Chanakya.

Tushar replied, "No" and started thinking.

He continued, "the credit of the trainees performance goes to their team leader, as the trainees join the team and get a better hands on experience through on the job training of actual sales."

"Right, but wasn't it the trainer, who did the heavy lifting and got the trainee to a level where he was ready to receive on the job training?" asked Chanakya.

"Yes", replied Tushar.

"Now let's look at another scenario, If a Biscuit company launches a new product, say a new flavor of cream biscuit, the marketing & advertising team plans, manages and implements the marketing & advertising campaign for the new cream biscuit. However, it is the sales team members who do the actual sales of the cream biscuits by interacting with the distributors and other channel partners. If the cream biscuit sells in high volume across geographies in a short span of time, who do you think gets the credit for its success, the marketing & advertising team or the sales team?" asked Chanakya.

"I strongly feel it is the advertising and marketing team, as they were the ones who drew the marketing and advertising plan across geographies." replied Tushar.

"Bingo! In both the cases of the bank and biscuit company, whose effort was visible? And whose outcomes are more visible?" asked Chanakya.

"The efforts are more visible for trainer's in the bank's case and the sales team member's in the biscuit company's case. While the outcomes are more visible for the team leader as they had direct authority over the trainees in the bank's case and marketing and advertising team members in the biscuit company's case as the impact was across the geographies." replied Tushar.

"Fair enough. Now that we have understood the dimension of higher visibility, let's move to the next one." said Chanakya.

# 3. Experimentation:

"Do you remember our discussion about the motivation spectrum from the afternoon?" questioned Chanakya.

"Yes, I do. Play, Purpose & Potential are positive motivators and Economic Pressure, Emotional Pressure and Inertia are negative motivators." replied Tushar.

"Good! Now tell me, if you had to make work playful for your team, what would you do?" asked Chanakya.

"I would gamify the work, like a treasure hunt." rejoined Tushar with a smile.

"That's an awesome idea!" complimented Chanakya.

He continued, "Now if you were to make work playful everyday and make your teammates tap dance to work, what would you do?"

Tushar started thinking. He then said, "I don't know. Can you help?"

"Of course." answered Chanakya.

He continued, "What do you think makes an activity playful vis-a-via boring?"

"The thrill", exclaimed Tushar.

"Okay and what is the source of thrill?" asked Chanakya.

"Maybe, the freedom to do things as you like, to achieve a goal," said Tushar.

"Ah that's interesting!" exclaimed Chanakya.

He continued, "That is precisely what creates play, it's referred to as experimentation. Experimentation is just like you said, the freedom to hit and try to achieve a goal. Now with this in mind Tushar, Do you think all jobs offer experimentation?"

"Some do. Most limit experimentation by having standard operating procedures". said Tushar.

"You are right." Now tell me, "Would you prefer a job with more experimentation or less?" enquired Chanakya.

"Of course, a job that offers more experimentation," said Tushar.

"Exactly. That's why jobs that have more experimentation are preferred." said Chanakya.

He continued, "Can you give a couple of examples of jobs that allow a lot of experimentation?"

"Event manager, Chef, Artist, Employee engagement professional, Content professional, Music composer etc", said Tushar enthusiastically.

"Wow! That's quite a list". said Chanakya.

He continued, "Can you give a couple of examples of jobs that allow very little to no experimentation?"

"Cashier, Probationary officer in a bank, Pilot, Operations team members, Assembly line workers, Factory supervisor, HR operations executive etc." said Tushar

He continued, "But when I think of it. Some people, with their creative mind, make the most mundane task experimentation for themselves, like the traffic police officer in Indore, who expresses himself through dance and controls the traffic, while entertaining people. So, I think most jobs which do not have experimentation embedded in them can be made interesting by thinking and acting creatively."

"That's an amazing insight!" complimented Chanakya.

He continued, "As you rightly pointed out the experimentation for a role varies from one case to another, even between the same roles in different scenarios. While some roles have innate experimentation built into them, there are others where experimentation can be enhanced through creativity."

# 4. Flexibility:

"Now let us understand the next dimension," said Chanakya.

He continued, "Do you value flexibility in a role, Tushar?"

"Yes. I would love to have a well paying job that can be done remotely from my native place." said Tushar.

"Well, remote is definitely a welcome flexibility in a job for a lot of people. However, the flexibility I am referring to is more intrinsic to the job or within a job." said Chanakya.

Tushar was confused. He asked Chanakya to shed some light on what he meant.

"Let me elaborate, remote or working from an office are two alternatives in any job and remote is a form of flexibility. However, there is another flexibility within a job, which is defined by time, before your work is evaluated." explained Chanakya.

Tushar got the idea, But he was still not fully clear. He said, "Can you help me understand this idea with a couple of examples?"

"Sure. Are you aware of the term SLA?" asked Chanakya.

"Are you referring to the SLA that is common in operational jobs like in data entry to enter certain quantum of data by a certain time daily, data operations to process a certain number of transactions by a certain time daily, call centers & BPOs to complete a certain number of interactions of a particular activity by a certain time daily?" asked Tushar.

"Yes! That's correct." replied Chanakya.

He continued, "What do you understand by an SLA?"

"It is essentially a certain percentage of a type of work that needs to be completed by a given time on a daily basis. Example-95% of all the data received by 6 am today needs to be processed by 6 pm the same evening. It is committed to the client." replied Tushar.

"That's comprehensive. So tell me what does an SLA driven role, do to the role?" asked Chanakya.

"It makes the role too operational in nature and a person doing the role feels more like a machine than a human. It takes the life out of a role." said a frustrated Tushar recalling his daily experience from his current role.

Chanakya sensed the frustration in Tushar's voice and said, "I understand you have a role that binds you to an SLA, makes you adhere to tight timelines and takes away any chance of creativity, experimentation and learning out of the role, making it monotonous."

He continued, "But like we discussed it helps to understand where we stand so that we can chalk out our future path from here. Staying stuck in a victim mindset, do you think it is going to help you in any way?"

"No." sighed Tushar.

"Then can we leave the emotion out of the equation and focus on understanding the framework? This understanding would in turn help you in discovering your customized career pathway that will put you on the runway for contentment, peace of mind and sustainable growth." said Chanakya.

"Yes. Thank you for helping me regain perspective." acknowledged Tushar.

"You are welcome! Okay. Now tell me does every role have an SLA or a recurring hard timeline daily?" asked Chanakya.

"A timeline is a part of every role. For some roles it is flexible. However, these roles do not have a recurring daily hard timeline or SLA to meet." answered Tushar.

"Great. Do you think having flexibility helps?" asked Chanakya.

"If the job is to produce a baby in 9 months, not having the expectation that 1/9th of the baby be produced every 1 month definitely helps. So of course it does help." said Tushar.

Chanakya burst out laughing.

He complimented, "That was some concentrated sarcasm used constructively to drive home your point!"

The compliment lightened the mood and got Tushar to relax.

Chanakya started, "You have already given examples of roles that have a recurring daily timeline or an SLA. Can you give me a couple of examples of roles that allow flexibility in the context we just discussed?"

"Sure. UI/UX developers, who develop the user interface or experience for a product, Product managers in an IT product company, who are involved in building a new product or an enhancement to an existing product, Employee engagement professionals, Learning and development professionals apart from inductions and regulatory training, etc." said Tushar.

"Fair enough. Now that you have understood the inbuilt flexibility in a role, appreciate its presence and are able to clearly identify roles that offer this benefit, let's move to the final dimension of our framework." said Chanakya.

## 5. Autonomy:

"This dimension is fairly straightforward." said Chanakya.

He continued, "Do you think all roles at the same level in the hierarchy have the same level of autonomy?"

"No. Some roles have more and some have less. It also depends on how delegating your Manager is." replied Tushar.

"You are absolutely on the point about the Manager. However, we will take that up in a little while. For now let's focus on autonomy that is built-in, in a role." said Chanakya.

He continued, "Why do you think some roles have more autonomy while others have less of it?"

Tushar thought for a while and continued, "I think it is for roles where one is accountable for the outcome and is free to choose the path one needs to take within lawful and rational bounds to achieve it."

He continued, "The accountability of the outcome combined with the autonomy to choose the interim course of action, inspires a sense of ownership in the individual. In my limited experience, I have seen people who take ownership in their work are likely to do better in life."

"That's insightful!" exclaimed Chanakya.

He continued, "Your insight is bang on. Accountability for outcomes and autonomy are a sustainable complement and both put together produce the elixir of ownership that aligns personal passion with the company's mission."

Chanakya then asked, "Can you think of a couple of roles that have built-in autonomy?"

"Designers, content curators, advertising professionals, marketing professionals, sales professionals to a degree." said Tushar.

"That sums it up!" said Chanakya.

"But I have a question," said a curious Tushar.

He continued, "When I think of the framework that you just laid out in front of me holistically and connect the dots, I see a significant overlap between high impact, high visibility, highly experimental, highly flexible and highly autonomous roles. In my mind, each of them represents a circle, I see all the circles overlapping significantly. Is my understanding correct?"

Chanakya smiled and said. "Yes, it is and like I said, you are a fast learner. The roles do overlap and such roles are called **Leverage roles**."

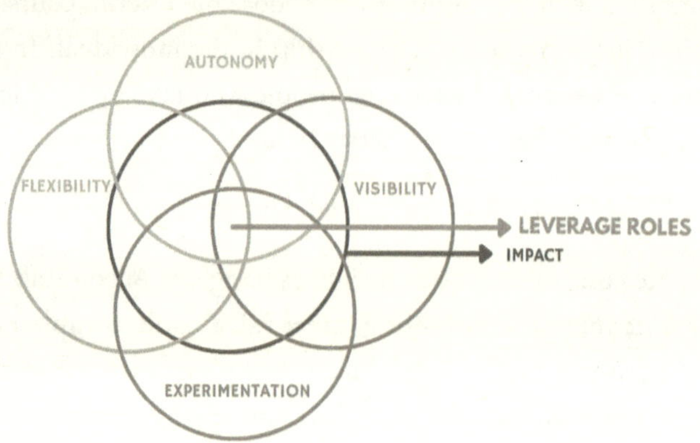


"In a nutshell, **Performance = Effort x Leverage**.[15] The effort you can put in, is capped. But your leverage is not. Higher your impact, visibility, experimentation, flexibility and autonomy as part of your role, higher your influence and hence your leverage." said Chanakya.

"That formula is a helpful way to hold this framework intact in memory." Thank you! said Tushar.

"You are welcome." mentioned Chanakya.

---

15. Reference: Inspired from the book, Catalyst by Chandramouli Venkatesan

He continued, "That's all there is to the framework. The five dimensions leading you to understanding what a leverage role comprises."

"But aren't you going to ask me to come up with examples for leverage roles?" retorted Tushar, as if he was anticipating the question and preparing an answer for the same in the back of his mind.

"I don't think that's needed. You have understood the components that make a leverage role. You now know the right questions to ask to categorize any role." replied Chanakya.

Tushar felt elated! Then suddenly he asked, "Shouldn't it be the right answers?"

Chanakya smiled and said, Wise is the one who asks the right questions, answers are within you."

"But what about the pay for the role? What does that depend on?" interrupted Tushar.

"Ah! Yes we will discuss pay after sometime. The equation of pay needs a few more inputs that you need to understand. We will discuss pay soon. Hold on to your question for a while. For now you are ready to customize and find your personal career path."

"But how can I decide on a role without knowing the pay?" asked Tushar.

Tushar immediately became conscious and replied to his own question. "I get it. That is how it should be. I based my decision on pay led by my social conditioning earlier. I do not want to repeat that mistake again."

Chanakya smiled and said, "Knowing about the pay is a fair question to ask. But it's wise to keep the analysis of the role and the price attached to it separate, combining both is the last step of decision making."

He continued, "You have become wiser, since yesterday."

# Chapter 6

# Narrowing Career Options

It was around 11.30 am in the morning, The train had come to a halt at a platform. Tushar & Chanakya went to the gate to explore the station, stretch their legs & see if they could find something interesting to eat. They discovered the station was Raigarh. They strolled the platform for a couple of minutes and stopped at a large outlet on the platform to buy some savories & beverages. The train started soon. Both of them came back to their seats and gorged on the savories, as the intense discussion had left them famished. While they were eating, the caterer came to take orders for lunch. Both ordered a veg meal. The caterer told them the food would arrive by 1.30 pm. Both were fine with that as their bellies had just been replenished. Then while slowly relishing their beverage, they continued their discussion.

Tushar started, "I feel enlightened with all the wisdom you have been showering on me since yesterday. I am not sure how but I intuitively think, I am now capable of choosing the right career for myself with your help in between."

Chanakya said, "I concur with you completely and hence it's you who will do most of the talking. I will just ask questions."

"A wise man just told me wisdom lies in asking the right questions." chuckled Tushar.

Chanakya smiled with contentment & humility and said, "Shall we begin then?"

"Sure", said Tushar.

"Can you summarize your personality, your strengths, your aspirations & your areas of interest?" asked Chanakya.

"Sure," said Tushar.

He opened his diary and started reading out,

## Personality:

**Source of energy:** Internal, Nature: Introverted

**Information processing:** Intuitive, connecting the dots type..

**Decision-making mechanism:** Feeling based

**Approach:** Methodical.

# Strengths:

1. Ability to abstract key drivers of a given situation.

2. Pattern recognition to match situations from memory.

3. Pattern recognition to come up with solutions from memory.

**Aspiration:** I have always wanted to be a strategist. I enjoy strategizing and seeing my strategy take roots and grow in the real world.

**Areas of interest:** cricket, generating actionable insights from data in business especially food business.

"That's comprehensive!" said Chanakya.

He continued, "Now with this in mind & the career landscape we discussed, what are the best 3 to 5 career options for you?"

"Cricket analyst, Management consultant or Strategy consultant, Strategy manager, Product manager in an IT product company, Brand strategist, Market research analyst, Credit Analyst, etc." Tushar replied.

"Wow! Looks like we have inverted your initial problem. Now you seem to be spoilt for choices." exclaimed Chanakya.

"Good problem to have, I believe," said Tushar with a beaming smile.

"Yes. Now that you have a list of roles which align with your personality, strengths, aspiration and interest. Let's zero down on the best for you & everyone involved." said Chanakya.

"Okay. But how?" asked an impatient Tushar.

"Well, that's simple, we will use another venn diagram?" said Chanakya with a wink.

"What do you mean?" asked Tushar.

"Have you heard of the concept of Ikigai?" Chanakya cross questioned.

"Ah okay. Are you referring to the venn diagram based on Japanese philosophy?" asked Tushar.

"Yes. That is exactly what I am referring to." confirmed Chanakya.

He continued, "Do you know what the term Ikigai means?"

"I guess it means why you exist," said Tushar.

"Yes it does." Said Chanakya.

He continued, "Iki' in Japanese means 'life,' and 'gai' describes value or worth. Your ikigai is your life purpose or your bliss. It's what brings you joy and inspires you to get out of bed every morning."

He further added, "I will tweak the diagram a little to add my perspective."

Chanakya then pulled the diary and started drawing. Once he was finished he passed it on to Tushar to have a look.

**Chanakya's Dream Career:**[16]

Tushar took a good look at the venn diagram. He gathered his thoughts and curiously questioned, "I understand why the profession should be an intersection of what I love the most, what I am best at and what I can be paid the highest for, but what is the need to include, what the world needs the most?"

---

16. Inspired from the book, Ikigai The Japanese Secret to a Long and Happy Life By Héctor García, Francesc Miralles

He continued, "If there is an opening for a role, it means the world needs it. Why bother checking if it is the most or the least?"

"Ah, that's a very interesting question!" exclaimed Chanakya.

He continued, "Are you familiar with Lord Krishna's story?"

"Very well. I would have heard it from my grandmother a hundred times at least. I have read it as part of my Hindi curriculum and watched it on television too." said Tushar.

"Very good!" replied Chanakya.

He added, "Do you think he was a successful human being?"

Tushar said, "Yes, one of the most successful human beings, who is said to have walked on earth."

"True. So, Why do you think he was so successful?" asked Chanakya.

"Because he was an avatar of Lord Vishnu." replied Tushar quickly.

"Well, that he was. But first he was a human being and due to his achievements he is considered to be an avatar of Lord Vishnu. The 8th Avatar of Lord Vishnu." said Chanakya.

He continued, "In crux, he was a man who went on to become God through his karmas and not the other way round."

He further asked, "Now with that in mind, what do you think made him so successful?"

Tushar thought for a while and then said, "Sorry, honestly, I don't know."

"That's okay." responded Chanakya.

He added, "It's because he followed the mantra of Dharma."

"Okay. By Dharma you mean being religious?" asked Tushar.

Chanakya smiled and said, "No. By Dharma I mean the principle of greater good."

Tushar understood the explanation literally, but not deeply enough and it was visible on his face.

Sensing the same, Chanakya went on to explain, "In a nutshell he always created a win-win for everyone involved in a situation, including himself and let the definition of everyone involve literally each and everyone."

He continued, "Even if you take a look around you in nature, you will observe, the most sustainable relationships are symbiotic relationships, ones that create win-win situations like the crocodile and the little birds that pick its teeth. The birds get food by picking the crocodile's teeth and the crocodiles get rid of the irritation of small pieces of flesh stuck between its teeth."

"Oh okay. That's an awesome and practical example to affirm the philosophy of Dharma." said Tushar.

He continued, "Now I understand why the circle of what the world needs the most is so important."

"Great! When you are doing something with all your heart, you might as well do the thing the world needs the most while getting paid for the same." said Chanakya.

He added, "Now let's explore the answer to what the world needs the most, that you can be rewarded for handsomely."

# Chapter 7

# Choosing A Rewarding Sense of Purpose

It was around 1.30 pm and the train had just reached Jharsuguda Junction. Since it was a junction, the train would stop for at least 10 minutes. Chanakya and Tushar decided to stretch their legs. They strolled the platform and bought some fruits. It was a sunny day and the sun was shining at its peak in the afternoon. Both soon felt the need to get back to the shade and comfort of their compartment and returned. On their return, they were greeted by a pantry boy, who had brought their lunch. Both of them were hungry. They wasted no time and started eating. The food was warm and tasty. Both of them agreed that the food standards had improved significantly in recent times. After finishing their lunch they washed their hands and settled in their seats sipping buttermilk that they had bought.

The intensive discussion had left their mind and body famished. They had recharged their bodies with the tasty food, but they needed to rest to recharge their mind. So, both of them hit their berths and fell asleep quickly.

When Tushar woke up this time, he found Chanakya sitting and sipping on his piping hot coffee. Tushar got down from his berth and freshened up. When he returned Chanakya handed him a cup of warm coffee. He quietly sipped coffee for sometime trying to come back from his deep relaxing sleep.

"Are you ready to discuss the most awaited part, pay?" asked Chanakya.

Tushar gently smiled and said, after discussing such deep topics intensely," I am neutral to discussing pay, which is quite surprising for me too."

"Good! Dispassionate state is the best state to discuss a topic like pay that evokes so many intense emotions."sSaid Chanakya.

He continued, "Tell me Tushar, Are all job roles at the same level paid equally?"

"No, A manufacturing employee is paid very differently than a marketing employee or an R&D employee, even when they are at the same job level." replied Tushar.

"Right. Why do you think that happens, Tushar?" questioned Chanakya.

"To be honest my instinct is to say because they require very different skill sets. But I don't think that is the answer after the discussion we have had. So, let me think." Said Tushar.

Tushar thought for a while and started, "I think it's the kind of impact they have that determines their pay. I think in general, leverage roles as we discussed would get paid better than non-leverage roles. I do not have the data experience of all High-impact roles that we discussed, but the ones that I have like a product manager, UI/UX designer, Management consultants etc, I would like to wager that leverage roles are paid better than non-leverage roles."

"Fair enough. Your insight has substance to it. With your limited data experience of pay, you have reached the right conclusion." said Chanakya.

He continued, "Now tell me, are all high impact roles at the same level paid the same?"

"No." said Tushar & started thinking.

"But I don't know why that happens?" Tushar added.

"No problem." said Chanakya.

He added, "let's try to understand this with an example, think of a few leverage roles that are paid significantly higher than others?"

"Data scientist." Tushar said quickly.

"Okay. Why do you think Data scientists are paid better than other high-impact roles?" asked Chanakya.

"I think because their impact is very significant & probably because it is hard to find a good data scientist," said Tushar.

"Okay. Let's for now leave the significance of impact and focus on; it's hard to find a good data scientist." said Chanakya.

He added, "Which means they are short in supply."

"Yes and the number of companies that are adding a data science team are increasing significantly after learning about the massive positive impact that the team can generate for business driving up their demand, which is being driven up faster than supply." said Tushar.

"Awesome!" exclaimed Chanakya.

He added, "Can you think of other such high-impact roles?"

"Yes, Artificial intelligence & Machine learning professionals." replied Tushar.

"Good! Can you name some from the manufacturing sector?" asked Chanakya.

"Maybe a product manager or product designer for electric vehicles," said Tushar.

"Nice!" exclaimed Chanakya.

He continued, "Do you think these roles will always be remunerated above the average of comparable high-impact roles?"

"No. Only till their demand-supply gap remains unbalanced." said Tushar.

"Great! So their pay disparity is a fad, not a permanent phenomenon." said Chanakya.

He further asked, "If that's the case, which parameter can help in deciding the ranking for pay for roles?"

"I think I know this," said Tushar.

"It's the impact that one has. The more the one to many impact, the wider the impact and the wider the impact, higher the reward for the role." added Tushar.

Surrounded by self doubt, he then asked, "Am I correct?"

"Bingo! Spot on!" exclaimed Chanakya.

Tushar felt a sense of relief and his confidence rose again.

"Now tell me Tushar, which industries should you be getting in?" asked Chanakya.

"Ones that can pay well." said Tushar.

He added, "Profitable companies that are growing."

"Wonderful!" exclaimed Chanakya.

"Let's focus on profitability first", Chanakya added.

He then asked, "What kind of companies are profitable?"

"Ones that have a great product, brand, distribution, are efficient, good management etc." replied Tushar.

"Wow, that's good. That reminds me you have done an MBA in finance. So let me ask you which are the major types of business models at a broad level?" asked Chanakya.

Ah! I know this. said Tushar.

He continued, "At a broad level there are two major types of business models [17]

---

17. Reference:Inspired from Warren Buffett's letters to shareholders of Berkshire Hathaway.

1. **Differentiator:** One where the offering is differentiated by either superior quality, brand, license, patent etc.

2. **Low-cost operator:** One where the production is done at the lowest cost in the industry and the business thrives on efficiency."

"That's comprehensive!" said Chanakya.

He then asked, "Which type of business model do you think is more likely to pay higher on average to employees?"

"I think the differentiator business model is likely to pay higher on an average to its employees, as they get to charge a premium for the superior quality, brand, patent, license etc compared to a low-cost operator business model where no stone is left unturned to get the last inch of efficiency possible. However, for key leverage roles even the low-cost operator business model would pay a premium, but such roles in such a business model would be few, very few." answered Tushar.

"That's absolutely correct!" exclaimed Chanakya.

He added, "I appreciate your critical thinking about the other alternative too."

He further added, "Now that we have figured out the right business model, let's focus on growth. Do you think a stable business is going to pay better or a high growth business,assuming all other parameters are equal?"

"I think a high growth business that is well funded or even better self sustainable is going to pay better." replied Tushar.

"You are right. I like your caveat of being well funded. It is especially important in today's growth at all cost mortality driven on the steroid of venture funds capital." said Chanakya.

"How will you identify a high-growth Industry?" asked Chanakya.

"Using the same principle that we used for roles, where demand for the product or service, far outstrips supply for the foreseeable future." replied Tushar.

"Good. You are learning quickly." said Chanakya.

"Now tell me once you have identified the industry, how will you choose, which company to work for in that industry?" asked Chanakya.

Tushar started thinking. He thought for a good 15 mins and said, "I am not sure."

"No worries. Let me help you. It would depend on the company's pay strategy." said Chanakya.

He added, "If you take salaries for a given role in an industry across companies and plot it on a graph, you will have a distribution with the highest salary being the 100th percentile. Now if you divide the 100th percentile into 4 equal parts you get 4 quartiles. You will have different companies paying their employees in different quartiles for that role as per their pay strategy."

He then asked, "Which companies do you think would pay in the middle of the distribution, say between the 25th to 66th percentile and which do you think would pay between 75th to 100th percentile?"

"Wow! I never thought there was so much science of establishing pay." Let me think.

He thought deeply about it and then started, "I think someone who is challenging an established leader and has a decent chance from a resource & market share standpoint will pay in the highest quartile that is between 75th to 100th percentile usually. While the current leader would pay between 25th to 66th percentile. This would happen especially for high-impact roles."

He further added, "I think this would happen as the challenger would benefit significantly from an economic standpoint if it is able to overthrow the existing leader and would hence have a more aggressive pay policy for high-impact roles that is targeted to attract quality talent. While the leader, however agile their history might have been, tends to get complacent as they do not have a lot to gain in terms of dominating the industry and is more likely to have a defensive pay strategy that is targeted to retain existing talent."

"That's insightful and correct!" exclaimed Chanakya.

He continued, "Now that we have understood what drives pay, tell me Tushar, Is a manufacturing company likely to pay better or a services company, assuming both have a differentiator business model?"

"This is fairly straightforward, a services company is likely to pay better as in its case the delivery of services depends on the employees making them a critical resource, plus such companies do not have to worry about raw material, inventory or manufacturing cost, which gives them the added purse to pay better. Also, these service companies would include internet based product companies." replied Tushar.

"Magnificent! We have discussed successfully everything that drives pay majorly." exclaimed Chanakya.

He added, "The pay principles we discussed apply in general to the whole workforce and become pronounced for high-impact roles."

"Why only high impact roles and not leverage roles?" asked a curious Tushar.

"Good question!" exclaimed Chanakya.

"The answer lies in the difference in perspective." He added.

Okay. Can you please elaborate?" asked Tushar.

"Sure. The other characteristics of leverage roles are intangible in nature and more beneficial to the employee directly. Yes, they do benefit the company significantly when they are practiced across the company by becoming part of their culture. Hence, the culture of the organization is the most valuable intangible asset that does not appear on the balance sheet of the company due to lack of its quantifiability." Said Chanakya.

"Oh okay. So, a leverage role is an employee specific thing." Said Tushar.

He added, "Now it makes total sense to me, why building a high performing culture is a sought after thing in the corporate world."

"I have another question, If the leader does not pay the top salaries to employees, why do their employees remain so loyal to these companies?" asked a confused Tushar.

"Ah that's a very interesting question!" exclaimed Tushar.

He continued, "the answer is the culture of the company."

"As companies become leaders and grow big, they change their focus from pay focussed talent attraction strategies to total reward focussed talent retention strategy. With the total reward focussed talent retention strategy they build a culture that promotes performance by promoting practice of company values, best practices, communication of vision and mission clearly across the company and providing benefits to employees instead of handing them cash in hand. This makes the existing employees feel at home and makes them stay for long periods, sometimes throughout their careers." He added.

"Okay. I never thought so deeply. This is amazing how the pay strategy varies based on different business models and life-stage of companies. Thank you so much." said Tushar.

"You are most welcome!" beamed Chanakya with his typical smile.

"Now let's choose a couple of your shortlisted options from our earlier discussion. Can you tell me what they were?" asked Chanakya.

"Sure. They are: Cricket Analyst, Strategy Consultant or Strategy Manager, Product Manager in an IT product company, Brand Strategist, Market Research Analyst, Credit Analyst." recalled Tushar.

"Fair enough. Now how do you wish to proceed to further narrow down your choices?" questioned Chanakya.

"I think to further shortlist, let's put to use the principle of exclusion, as the shortlisted list has options that I like and it would be difficult for me to choose one of them, while keeping my emotions out of the equation." said Tushar.

"Good idea!" exclaimed Chanakya.

"Let's start!", He added.

"Sure. Let's start with Cricket Analyst. I think cricket has a bright future in our country & across the globe, but consider the number of people who are passionate, hungry and trying to get into the ecosystem as a cricket analyst. The competition is high. This creates an oversupply of people aspiring for the role, thereby reducing the potential chance to get into the role." said Tushar.

"Dispassionate indeed!" exclaimed Chanakya.

"Moving on, Product manager in an IT product company would require a technical background and hence I will need to acquire a new skill. Acquiring new skills is a good thing and I would have loved to do it. However, venturing into an altogether unrelated territory without a real prospect in hand does not seem like a good idea. So that too is ruled out." muttered Tushar.

"Sounds reasonable. Let's move to the next one." said Chanakya.

"Brand Strategist is something I would love to do, but getting into the role of a brand strategist at this point in my career without any related experience or education would be practically not possible. However, I would love to do this sometime in the future, when I can afford to take risks and people recognize this skill of mine. So, for now it is ruled out." said Tushar.

"Smart move! When you can't win the battle, postpone it to a day when you can and then fight it." rejoined Chanakya.

"Moving on, Market Research Analyst, though I am good at drawing actionable insights, my knowledge of statistical tools and programs is limited. Learning the same would require investing significant time & resources and venturing into learning this unrelated skill with nothing tangible in hand does not sound like a great idea, so this too is ruled out." said Tushar.

"Okay let's have the remaining two, Strategy Consultant or Strategy Manager & Credit Analyst to eliminate and come to a choice for the next step." said Chanakya.

He continued, "Now tell me, which of the two roles namely, Strategy Consultant or Strategy Manager & Credit Analyst would the world need more?"

"That's a tough question. Let me think." Tushar started thinking.

After thinking for a good 10 minutes, he said, I think the world needs both, Strategy Consultant or Strategy Manager help in making a business effective & efficient and help in scaling the business, while Credit Analysts, help banks and other lending institutions in deciding if a borrower is creditworthy and can be given credit.

"Hmmm. I agree with you that it is difficult to base your decision on this question. As both roles have a wider impact. However, I think as a Credit Analyst you are likely to evaluate and ensure allocation of resources to more businesses than as a Strategy Consultant, simply because businesses of all sizes are looking for getting loans, especially with the recent ease of doing business and democratization of credit. Whereas there are fewer companies in India that hire a Strategy Consultant, simply due to lack of awareness of its benefits and sometimes due to unwillingness to give away control. A Strategy Consultant works for a single company and enables the efficiency, effectiveness and scaling of one business. Yes, if the business goes on to become a multinational corporation, your impact might be larger in that case." said Chanakya.

"That sounds like a very logical and practical argument. I agree with it." mentioned Tushar.

"Great. Let's not finalize the career now, as we need to add another dimension to the current picture to make it holistic and that is time or longevity." said Chanakya.

"Okay and what do we need to do for that?" asked a curious Tushar.

"Visualize where you want to see yourself in the future and ascertain which of the options would be most skill or resource developing for you to get there." explained Chanakya.

He continued, "But before that let's have some fresh fruits! I am starving again."

# Chapter 8

# Viewing Career – An Unfolding Movie or Still Photograph

Once they finished having fruits, they cleaned themselves and the seat and then settled down.

Tushar started, "I have a question."

He continued, "Why can't I start by answering the question, what does the world need the most? Don't you think I will get to capitalize on my natural gifts the most?"

"Ah, that's a very interesting perspective!" exclaimed Chanakya.

He continued, "You can do that when you already have more than enough resources."

"But by asking what is best for me first, am I not being selfish? Isn't that wrong?" asked Tushar.

"Not at all. You can only pour from a filled cup. You are just filling the cup first and then emptying it." said Chanakya.

He added further, "One only needs to shift from filling the cup to emptying it like many greats in the past did, once you have more than enough. These include great businessmen like Bill Gates, Warren Buffett, J.R.D Tata, Dhirubhai Ambani, Azim Premji etc. All these great businessmen first accumulated wealth and then once they had more than enough, they built a longer table instead of a higher wall to give it back to the society."

"Thank you! That has resolved all my doubts about the sequencing." said Tushar.

Tushar paused and then said, "However, now I have another question. All the great people that you gave examples of have been businessmen or investors, none of them were in a job all their life. How do you think I can pull it off with a corporate job?"

"Who said you are going to do this job or any job for the rest of your professional career!" said Chanakya.

"Well, I don't know. I have not thought of a business, but investing in businesses is something that interests me. However, I am not sure if I would be able to spare enough to build a fortune. Do you think I can?" asked Tushar.

"Of course you can! But first you need to believe you can." said Chanakya.

"Truly speaking emotionally I can believe, but with the small savings that I am able to save, logically it looks improbable." said Tushar.

"Well, firstly it's not where you are that defines you, but where you can and will go that does. Secondly, no amount is small to build a fortune." said Chanakya.

He continued, "To elaborate on my second point, imagine your savings to be a small snowball, in order to build a fortune, all you need is a snow filled hill, whose slope is long & steep enough for the snowball to become massive."

"That's an interesting corollary!" exclaimed Tushar.

Chanakya further added," In a career just like in investment, your direction and time are more important than your speed. Yes, your initial position matters and starting a business early has its advantages. However, it also has pitfalls. When you start early you are naive and your naivety ends up costing you through bad decisions, leading to potential early setbacks. Whereas when you start with the right kind of experience, your decision quality improves and you save yourself from consequences of potential bad decisions. In essence by starting late with the right experience you make up for the head start with improved decision quality."

"In fact, all the people that I just mentioned did work for someone else and only over a period in time did they evolve into the version of their personality that the world is most familiar with. For example, Warren Buffett delivered newspapers as a kid, collected used golf balls that he could sell and worked for his mentor Benjamin Graham as an employee before starting on his own. Dhirubhai Ambani worked as a petrol bunk attendant before starting on his own, Bill Gates worked at Honeywell as a computer programmer before starting on his own." said Chanakya.

"Awesome! That makes things crystal clear for me and gives me conviction to follow this pattern." said Tushar.

"Nice. Pattern is the word that you need to understand thoroughly to think about a career holistically." said Chanakya.

"Okay. Could you elaborate?" said Tushar.

"Sure. You need to visualize the sub parts of your career that may include any or all of the following, different roles in corporates, from being a professional, to being a businessman, to being an investor. You need to have a sense of why you are doing something & how this sub part is going to help you in your whole career. In a nutshell, Career, my friend, is to be viewed like an unfolding movie, not a still photograph." said Chanakya.

"Wow! That's a very interesting perspective and I will remember the movie not photograph corollary for my life. Thank you so much." said Tushar filled with gratitude.

"You are welcome," said Chanakya with contentment.

"Wait a minute, you said, Look at a career like a movie, not a still photograph. Sometimes we don't know the exact movie that we want to have? In that case how do we navigate ourselves in the uncertain world?" asked Tushar.

"Well, that's why I said an unfolding movie and not a pre-directed one." Chanakya replied with a wink.

He added, "Relax! Most people do not have it all figured out on day one or even by the middle of their career journey. The blueprint does not exist at the beginning, but evolves over time. You make it as you move ahead in your career. It is a very much alive & iterative process. It's a verb, not a noun. All you need is a clear compass."

"Okay. What does that compass look like?" asked a curious Tushar.

Chanakya smiled and said, "It consists of answering 2 simple questions:

1. What space of mind am I approaching this current role?

2. Is this role going to help me develop a skill or resource that is going to add value to my long-term career?

Being crystal clear about these is really important. As it's really important for you to come from a happy, grateful & abundant state of mind and not from a space of guilt, pressure, shame or any other negative space. Also it is really important that your current role be value accretive in the long run for your career, either in the form of a skill or resource."

"Amazing! That's very helpful." said Tushar.

"However, you must always try to get an idea of the career destination, where you want to end up in your career," said Chanakya.

He added, "By that I do not mean the exact business, role or profession or quantum of wealth or type of house etc, but to have a clear understanding of how you want to feel by the time you reach the end of your career. You can obviously add more details to it over time as the idea of the career destination."

"This sounds like a practical idea," said Tushar.

"I have always thought about the suggestion I kept getting from my elders that you must have a clear career destination to move ahead in your career. I always wondered, How can I know about my career destination with precision, when I myself am exploring the world? The idea of how I want to feel at my career destination resolves that question." He added.

"Yes, you can make a vision board about your vision in life and make it clearer by evolving it over time as you gain clarity with experience." said Chanakya.

"I have heard about a vision board. But I was always skeptical on how to make it. Thank you for reminding me. Will you help me with that?" asked Tushar."

"Sure, I will. But right now, let's come back to the next most important part of the role, choosing a good Boss." replied Chanakya.

# Chapter 9

# Choose A Boss, Not A Job

Tushar started, "How is choosing a good boss so important for my career? Isn't the boss an external factor? And going by all we have discussed, you have emphasized the most on internal factors like motivation, independence of thought etc, why a sudden shift to an external factor?"

"That's quick critical thinking!" exclaimed Chanakya.

He then asked, "How important do you think the role of a teacher is in your life?"

He further added, "Don't be in a hurry to reply. Think about it for sometime while we enjoy a cup of coffee."

The coffee vendor had just arrived. He handed over a cup of coffee each to Tushar and Chanakya. Chanakya requested to make his coffee strong and the vendor added more coffee powder to make the coffee stronger. Both sat quietly sipping their coffee.

Tushar after quite some contemplation of his childhood, teenage and college life was ready with his answer. He started,

"All my teachers taught me the respective subjects, but a special few also taught me the importance of good values and how those values should get reflected in our behavior. They helped me develop self belief and empowered me to think for myself, instead of dictating what was right and what was wrong. They shaped my attitude and outlook towards life for good. Now that I think of this, I have nothing but gratitude for the special ones, who went beyond the call of duty in shaping my character & personality."

"Okay. Do you see any parallels between a teacher in your educational life and a boss in your corporate life?" Asked Chanakya.

Tushar took a pause. Thought for a while and said, "Now that I think of it, I do see a parallel."

He added, "My experience with my manager never made me feel so. She treats me like I am a lifeless machine, whose only job is to finish the work as per her expectations."

He further added, "However, I have seen a couple of my colleagues have great rapport with their manager. Their manager treats them in a friendly way and teaches them things by hand-holding them, when a task is new and then letting them be on their own once they have learned the basics."

"That's a very handy experience from our discussion standpoint!" exclaimed Chanakya.

He added, "Have you noticed any difference in your friends who have a supportive manager?"

"Yes! They have grown into significantly more confident individuals and have transformed from freshers to dependable professionals. It has made them bolder in taking decisions and being accountable for them. It has also made them more experimental as their manager does not ask them to walk his/her talk like a horse with blinders." replied Tushar.

"Great observations!" exclaimed Chanakya.

He added, "One of the most important factors that can catalyze your career for good is a good Boss."

He then asked, "Now do you see how much difference can a good Boss make in a professional's life, especially early in life?"

"Yes. I do. That's very helpful, thank you!" replied Tushar.

He then added, "But I don't understand, if I could sense it in my short stint at corporates, can't the top management understand this and act on it? I see the not so manager-employee relationship to be the most common issue in corporates. The ones who are lucky to have a good boss are a handful of individuals. Most employees have an experience similar to mine."

"Very true. Human resource is the most misallocated resource around, especially at managerial level. In my opinion, by simply reallocating human resources at managerial level, India could add a couple of percentage points extra to our GDP growth rate and can reach its economic growth goals 10 to 15 years before. This would not just lead to economic prosperity but to social prosperity too as it would enable a lot of talented people to unleash their full potential, whose impact socially would be material." replied Chanakya.

"Exactly, then why don't top management at companies do something about it?" questioned a desperate Tushar.

"Well, the top management in the best companies actually put a lot of emphasis on this while inculcating and maintaining their corporate culture. They have rigorous behavioral assessments that an employee needs to pass through before they can become a Manager. In such companies being a good performer alone is not enough to let someone into the managerial role." replied Chanakya.

"That's great! But in my limited experience, I don't see many companies follow this kind of assessment before promoting someone to a managerial role. In what I have seen, either promotions are handed out to the best performer or to someone who survives in a company while their colleagues have moved to other companies. Is my experience set at the middle of the corporate pyramid or at its bottom?" asked Tushar.

Chanakya smiled and said, "It is very much in the middle. You are right, most companies promote either their best performers or the senior most who are left after all the people of a certain level have moved to other companies or hire someone from another company from the same level or a junior level with little or no consideration for their attitude or managerial ability."

"I fail to understand why the top management does not address such a visible problem in the bulk of the companies." fumed Tushar.

"The answer lies in inertia," said Chanakya.

He added, "Companies often become complacent as they grow and accept mediocrity. They then fall prey to social beliefs of taking technical good performance as a proxy for prospective good managerial performance or lay too much emphasis either on experience or on the wisdom of the new hire's previous employer. The subjective assessment of managerial fitment makes the practice easier to accept. Quite often the top management that runs the show too has climbed the ladder over the years following similar methods and are not bold enough or radical enough to challenge the status quo."

"Hmmm. That's deep and a structural issue. Thanks for patiently explaining it." said Tushar.

"You are welcome," said Chanakya.

He continued, "Now that you have understood the importance of a good boss and why bad bosses are so common. Shall we figure out what kind of a Boss is a good one and how to identify them?"

"Sure. This sounds very useful and interesting." said Tushar.

"Fair enough. Tell me Tushar, what qualities make a Manager a good boss?" asked Chanakya.

"Okay. I think a Manager has following qualities:

1. Cares about their people

2. Respects them for who they are

3. Allows them freedom to experiment, make mistakes & learn from those mistakes

4. Someone who tells what to achieve, but does not get too much into how to do it, unless the task is new or the team member has asked for help.

5. Someone who stands for his team members & advocates their wellbeing.

6. Someone who appreciates them genuinely for their efforts.

7. Someone who inspires open communication & collaboration within the team.

8. Someone who knows the art of making a not so interesting task interesting.

9. Someone who leads from the front and does not shy away from getting their hands dirty in execution if need be.

10. Someone who uses positive motivators and not negative ones.

11. Someone who is fair, just and measures themselves with the same scale they use for others.

12. Someone who understands each of their team members and treats them as they would like to be treated in their own customized way.

Basically a good boss is one who does not boss around all the time. Are my expectations realistic or out of a fairy tale?" asked Tushar.

Chanakya laughed and said, "Well, such people are rare but they do exist. Between you have identified very good traits. I can shorten it by consolidating, but I would want it to be Tushar's original expectations and will not tamper with the list. Good job!"

"Thank you!" said Tushar.

He continued, "But how do I identify them? Sometimes we don't get to meet our Manager in the interview and meet them the day we join."

"Well, the answer to that question lies in asking the right question to the talent acquisition manager and doing your own R&D." said Chanakya.

"Okay. Could you elaborate?" asked Tushar.

"Sure. Ask your Talent Acquisition Manager for your Manager's name. Go search them on social media. Dig out all the information you can about them that is publicly available. Once you have everything in place, request the Talent Acquisition Manager to arrange for a 1:1 discussion with your prospective manager. Explain to them that your decision to join crucially hinges on who your Manager is going to be." said Chanakya.

"Okay. But do you think the Talent Acquisition Manager is going to entertain my request? I mean, I am not in a position to negotiate on this." said Tushar.

"Well, you very much are. Always remember Tushar, You can negotiate with anyone. Do not give away your negotiation power by losing it in your mind." said Chanakya.

"But how do I find if my Manager has the qualities I listed above in just one meeting?" asked Tushar.

"That would require you to learn to read people. With your intuitive mind & proper practice you can become good at it. You do not need answers to all the questions, but to get the right vibe from the way the person interacts. You will make mistakes, but I can assure you with practice you will get better at reading people." said Chanakya.

He added, "You can additionally get the names of your team members from the Talent Acquisition Manager and also request for a meeting. In the meeting you can talk to people from the team that you are going to join and find out about the management style. You will need to learn the art of asking seemingly trivial questions to gauge the team environment, which will give you an idea about your prospective manager's management style."

"Okay." replied Tushar. But he was still unsure if the idea would work and his facial expression revealed the same.

"There might be instances where you will not get all the inputs either because the social media profiles are locked or the Talent Acquisition Manager is reluctant in arranging the meetings stating that the manager and team members are busy or both. If you hear the latter reason, even after multiple requests, you would be better off declining that offer. Probabilistically there is a chance that people might be genuinely busy. But then, if neither of them consider it important enough to meet a prospective team member, it would be safe to give the opportunity a pass." explained Chanakya.

"I totally agree with the approach. But don't you think this would lead to a lot of forgone opportunities?" asked a desperate Tushar.

"Yes, it would lead to forgoing a lot of opportunities that are most likely not worthy from your best interest perspective," said Chanakya.

He added, "Plus you are not a fresher or in desperate need of a job. Your aim is not just to secure a higher package, but to do something worthwhile that adds value beyond money, in terms of skills, relationships and learning."

He further added, "Always remember, the decision to leave one company and join another company is not one but two separate decisions. You need to treat them separately unless you are in desperate need of a job. It is wise to jump ship only when you are sure that the next ship is better."

"That's insightful! Treating the two decisions separately unlike how most people do. I will keep that in mind." said Tushar.

"Good. Also remember, a bad job with a good boss is better than a good job with a bad boss." said Chanakya.

"That sounds paradoxical but I intuitively know it is true. The relation between the boss and employee is the most important professional relationship for the employee as this relationship shapes an employee's immediate work environment. Hence I can see the merit in your finding." said Tushar.

He then asked, "Now that you have laid out everything in front of me & made me capable enough to see my dream job, please also tell me how to find one?"

"Sure. But first let's order dinner. The pantry boy is here already." said Chanakya.

# Chapter 10

# Manifest Your Dream Job

The time was around 7.30 pm and the train had stopped at Chakulia, a small town in Jharkhand. Both Chanakya and Tushar thought of getting out to get some fresh air. But before they could get down, the train began to move. Both took a walk till the pantry car crossed various compartments, had a cup of tea each and returned to their seats.

On their return Chanakya started, "Tell me Tushar, do you think dream roles exist in finished form?"

"I think they do." replied Tushar.

"So many people who aspire to become high-ranking officials in the government end up doing so. I think they dream of doing so early in life. So I think dream jobs exist and some people get to live their dream job." He added.

"Fair enough. But what percentage of people end up in their initially thought stereotypical dream job like a high-ranking government official or end up getting a job in their dream company? What happens to those who do not end up where they initially thought? Don't they ever get to their dream job?" asked Chanakya.

"Well, very few actually get their stereotypical dream job. The rest who do not get their dream job immediately, I don't know what happens to them to be honest. Can you tell me what happens, from your experience?" asked a confused Tushar.

"Okay. Most of them end up doing something productive with their lives and quite often end up where they thought they wanted to be at an abstract level. They end up feeling similar to what they had initially aspired for intently." said Chanakya.

"To be honest, dream jobs exist only in slam books in finished form for most people. Actually, most people have to carve them out of stone like a sculpture carves out idols from stones. Just here instead of hammer and chisel, you choose consciously, put focussed effort and most importantly have patience throughout the process." He added.

"That sounds practical. Not fancy and rags to riches kind of pattern, but a more real and practical one." said Tushar.

"Indeed. Reality is often different from expectation. It has its own randomness that appears orderly in hindsight." said Chanakya.

"On that note, contrary to the fairy tale where you land up in your dream job straight, in reality you take what you have, work at it, earn a living, while you keep moving towards your dream in a conscious manner. The direction of your movement is more important than speed." He added.

"Okay. Could you explain it to me with an example?" asked Tushar.

"Sure. Say I always wanted to be an investor, career counselor & business strategist. But when I did not have the skills, resources & opportunity to do that right after my education. So when I completed my education, my first job was of an analyst, I learned how to analyze businesses which is a critical part of investing, I then started teaching in finance in colleges, where I got to experiment with my teaching and acquire skills to apply as a career counselor by guiding my students, then I joined as a trainer in a company where I got a chance to practice and make myself perfect with the training delivery process as the content was more or less similar over multiple iterations, then I got to initiate, lead the learning & development department based on what my HR head saw in me while I was training employees. There I got to learn mentoring, project management, implementing strategies etc. All the while I kept saving and investing every penny I could, improvising & making my investing process better to earn my financial freedom. I finally was able to do that 10 years into corporates. That is when I started my independent career counseling and business strategy practice. The transition took some time, but with time, conscious strategy & effort things fell in place. Today I am living my professional dream, tap dancing to work every single day of my life." said Chanakya.

"The journey wasn't easy, but it was full of adventure and I thoroughly enjoyed the process." He added.

"The point I am trying to make is, you are the architect of your professional dream, you need to make the best of what you have and keep moving towards your dream with consciousness accumulating skills & resources and trust that if you get the process right, the opportunity or the proceeds will eventually follow. You need to have a constructive mindset throughout the process, especially when things are not working out best for you. Remember, your ability decides where you begin, but it is your attitude that determines where you end up." He further added.

"Words of wisdom and practice!" exclaimed Tushar.

"Another piece of practical advice is to have a set of core values and live by them, not just in words but in spirit. Your colleagues will remember you for how you made them feel at a given point in time and that depends on your behavior, which inturn depends on your values. Living by values like honesty, justice, timeliness, fairness etc is a good idea. But feel free to choose the ones that resonate the most with you." suggested Chanakya.

"That is profound. It reminds me of Maya Angleou's quote, People will forget what you said, people will forget what you did, but they will remember how you made them feel." quoted Tushar.

He then asked, "But how do I take the first step in that direction, that is, how do I find the job of a credit analyst that we shortlisted?"

"That is a good question! Let's brainstorm to find the best solution." replied Chanakya.

He continued, "What do you do now when you want to look for a certain kind of a role in the market?"

"I post my resume on job sites and keep updating my profile to stay on top of the search result and wait for the right recruiter to find me." replied Tushar.

"Okay. Why do people rely on job sites to get a job offer?" asked Chanakya.

"Obviously, because it is the marketplace for jobs." replied Tushar.

"True. But does that remain a marketplace for jobs you are looking for throughout your career?" asked Chanakya.

"I guess so." replied Tushar.

"Okay tell me, which is the best form of publicity?" asked Chanakya.

"Word of mouth." replied Tushar.

" Correct! Well, then shouldn't it be similar for getting a job?" asked Chanakya.

"Ya. I guess. But how? I am not so extroverted when it comes to going out and networking with people." replied Tushar.

"Well, networking surely helps. But there are other ways too. You can put your work out in the open for people to view." said Chanakya.

He then asked, "But that can't be done as it violates confidentiality, right?" asked Tushar.

"I did not mean that way. You can always showcase your learning by writing blogs, posts, making videos, doing podcasts and giving talks targeting potential employers." replied Chanakya.

He added, "In fact even if you do it with the sole purpose of expressing yourself. You would attract the right kind of people in the long run and might get a job offer."

"Wow. That's an interesting idea. I never thought about it this way. Thank you!" said Tushar.

"You are welcome!" Said Chanakya.

"By an estimate, 80% of the job market at an experienced level is hidden and it still works the old fashioned way by word of mouth referral. In fact even as a fresher, word of mouth can get you the right job offer." said Chanakya.

He continued, "Put yourself out in the world in places where you are exposed to chances for positive surprises. Keep trying as extreme career success is a black swan kind of event."

"Okay. Places like?" asked Tushar.

"Places where you can present your skill through your work sample to people like blogs, professional networking sites, panel discussions, conferences related to the industry you are targeting, volunteer for relevant industry associations etc. Also put your profiles on places like job sites, professional networking applications, start-up networking apps etc." replied Chanakya.

He added, "When you present your skills through your work sample, put up an unrelated work sample like writing an article about an interesting topic in your work area with nuances of how to apply in a generic manner."

He further added, "While making your profile from a professional perspective make it a point to write outcome and impact oriented statements, while giving a teaser on the how to execute part."

"Okay. That's very helpful. Thank you!" said Tushar.

He then asked, "Could you give me an example of an outcome or impact oriented statement?"

"Sure. Say if you prepared a guideline that helped the teams increase their productivity. You would say, Improved productivity by certain quantum by drafting a crucial operational guideline. Instead of saying, put x number of hours in developing a certain guideline." replied Chanakya.

He then asked, "if you were a Recruiter, which of the two statements is more likely to appeal to you?"

"The first one, the impact oriented one." replied Tushar immediately.

"Exactly my point". said Chanakya.

"Communication is an evergreen skill that can act like leverage for your other technical skills." He added.

Hmmm. True. Never thought that way. murmured Tushar.

"I have a question, If you say communication is an evergreen skill, is there another category of skills that are not evergreen?" Tushar asked.

"Ah. That's a pertinent question!" exclaimed Chanakya.

"So, I divide skill into two categories, they are evergreen & transitory. Evergreen as the name suggests are skills that are always in demand, they were in demand during your great grandfather's times and very likely will remain in demand during your great grandchildren's times. These skills are more fundamental in nature & are like compound interest, they snowball over time. Whereas Transitory skills are more of a fad like fashion, that come and go. They remain in high demand for a certain period and then the oversupply takes over." added Chanakya.

"Okay. This is new. Could you give me a few examples of each of the categories?" asked Tushar excitedly.

"Ya, sure. Let's start with evergreen skills. Leadership, organized thinking, numerical fluency, critical thinking, problem solving, analyzing, strategic thinking, systematic execution, team work, time management, project management, managing wealth etc are few of the evergreen skills. Also communication is a blanket evergreen skill that includes communication, interpretation, presentation, writing, story-telling etc. Many of these skills are referred to as soft skills." said Chanakya.

"Coming to transitory skills, these include everyday skills like learning a new coding language for a software developer, learning how to operate a company's internal system, learning how to operate a system or a machine, learning Microsoft excel or Microsoft office suite etc. Such skills are required for a person to execute their respective responsibilities & remain in use till the tool or machine remains relevant." He added.

"Wow! This is amazing. I never thought there could be a difference in lifespan of skills too. Doesn't it make more sense to master evergreen skills first?" asked Tushar.

"It does, unless there is an immediate requirement for you to learn a transitory skill to finish a job." replied Chanakya.

"Most evergreen skills have a compounding nature and grow better like wine with time. Also since they act as leverage to the rest of your skills, the benefits of investing time & energy in learning them first is definitely a wise course of action." He added.

"Right. I will make a customized list of each type for my own reference." said Tushar.

"Sure you can. However, I would always suggest you go back to the first principle of asking the category of the skill by applying the definition. This way you will be able to remain agile and free from biases in gauging the type of skill." said Chanakya.

"Hmmm. That sounds like a good idea. Thanks!" said Tushar.

"You are welcome," said Chanakya.

"Another key area I would like you to understand is converging expectations with reality." added Chanakya.

"I see a lot of youngsters coming to the industry with the expectation that they would start doing high impact work from day one. Tell me honestly, did you think like this too?" He asked.

"Yes, I did think that way." replied Tushar sheepishly.

"But the reality turned out to be quite the opposite, it hit me very hard at an emotional level, made me feel like a modern peasant." added Tushar.

"I can understand. What do you think led you to feeling that way?" asked Chanakya.

"As a country we do a lot of back office work, owing to the labor arbitrage scenario. In India you could pay the fraction of salary that you would pay in a developed country to get trivial back office jobs done. I think that's the reason." said Tushar.

"Good point!" exclaimed Chanakya.

"However, even if we had all front office roles, I don't think this problem would perish." added Chanakya.

"Then what's the reason for the expectation-reality mismatch?" asked Tushar.

"Well, it is the expectation itself." replied Chanakya.

"For example, Studying corporate finance, we inherently assume we are going to make high impact corporate finance decisions from day one, studying marketing we assume we will be devising marketing strategy from day one and so on. While in reality we start by playing a smaller role in the whole scheme of things. Also, the placement & recruitment industry leaves no stone unturned to pump our expectations further." added Chanakya.

"It would be emotionally much easier if people came into jobs with lower expectations and an open mind to learn and be willing to get their hands messy in order to learn and climb the ladder." He further added.

Tushar after some contemplation said," That is a very simple, yet powerful idea to avoid self caused misery."

"Here comes dinner!" smiled Chanakya.

The time was around 9.30 pm and the train had stopped at a station, it was Jaleshwar, a small town in Odisha. The intense discussion had left both of them famished. Both of them washed their hands and sat to have dinner. The food was simple yet delicious.

By the time they finished the time was 10 pm and the train had stopped at Balasore. This was a relatively larger station. Both of them got down to stretch their legs. The sky was clear and it was breezy, the perfect weather to take a post dinner walk.

Tushar had received a lot of wisdom from Chanakya over the last two days. He, with his intuitive mind absorbed like a sponge. However, it was overwhelming too. Still his curiosity was not showing any signs of lethargy. This curious attitude of Tushar was the one that sparked the discussion and got Chanakya to pour his wisdom continuously over the last couple of days. Both of them walked quietly as if trying to cherish the intense discussion.

The train's siren jolted them out of their silence. They soon boarded the train as it began to move. Both of them returned to their seats. Tushar sat down as if, intuitively trying to tell Chanakya to continue their discussion. Chanakya sensed it. As much Chanakya appreciated Tushar's curiosity, he was also aware that the only thing Tushar needed right now is some me time for his subconscious mind to process the intense discussion they had.

I am feeling tired and sleepy, I have to get down at Bhubaneswar where the train reaches at 1.45 am. So, it would be best if we retire for the night. said Chanakya.

"Yes, sure." replied Tushar.

Both of them set up their beddings and went off to bed, bidding good night to each other.

Tushar felt guilty for prolonging the discussion, which meant Chanakya would get less sleep as he was to disembark at Bhubaneswar at 1.45 am. He was touched by Chanakya's generosity and willingness to share wisdom unconditionally. He had never met anyone like Chanakya before in his life. His presence had made him feel secure and he had begun to believe in himself again. He thought, what a journey it had been! He came to enjoy a vacation, but ended up discovering himself and gaining insights on how he could construct his dream from the ground up brick by brick. He was in complete awe of Chanakya and had immense gratitude for him. Chanakya was a teacher, true to his name, he thought and fell asleep.

When he woke up due to the lights. Suddenly a lot of movement started in their compartment. He checked the time, it was 1.30 am. He quickly got down from his seat. He found Chanakya sitting there with his luggage ready, sipping his coffee.

"Good morning!" said Tushar.

"Very good morning! I thought I would leave you a note as you were in deep sleep." said Chanakya.

"I was indeed. But I am glad I woke up." said Tushar.

He continued, "I have to ask you something, a last question. Can I?"

"Of course you can Tushar. Go on!" replied Chanakya with a warm smile.

"Why me Chanakya?" asked Tushar

"Why did you choose to share your wisdom with me?" He added.

Chanakya smiled with warmth & said, "You choose a student for his heart."

He added, "You have a selfless one."

"But I am not without my selfish motives!" exclaimed Tushar.

"Selflessness cannot exist without selfishness, Tushar," said Chanakya.

He added, "In fact, selflessness & selfishness are sides of the same coin."

While Tushar was trying to comprehend the statement in its entirety, the train began to slow down. Bhubaneswar station had arrived. Tushar helped Chanakya with his luggage. The train stopped and they disembarked.

"So, that's it?" asked Tushar with moist eyes.

"Well, it's just the beginning, my friend of a deep lifelong friendship. I hope you will accept me as your friend. Would you?" asked Chanakya with warmth in his voice.

Tushar couldn't contain himself and hugged Chanakya and said gladly, "It would be an honor".

The train's siren reminded Tushar, it was time to say goodbye. He had never been good with goodbyes. He embarked the train and waved at Chanakya till his vision became blurry.

Tushar returned to his seat and felt the need for a face wash. He washed his face and returned to his seat. All of a sudden a thought struck him, he had not taken Chanakya's contact nor had he shared his with him. He started feeling dumb. How could he have missed something so trivial.

Alas he felt the need to sleep. Puri was an hour and a half journey from Bhubaneswar. As he lay down, he found an envelope on his pillow. It had a note that read,

*Dear Tushar,*

*It was a pleasure interacting with you.*

*By the time you find this, I would have left, but I would love for us to stay in touch as friends. If you are willing to accept the gift of my friendship.*

*Remember Tushar, Everything in life can be attained with clarity of intent and strategy. Intent is the heart of anything and everything we do. Strategy is how you get from where you are to where you want to be. Strategy is rooted in inner power, which comes from self-belief. So, never ever stop believing in yourself.*

*One request, all the wisdom we received as a result of our discussion, make it a point to pay it forward to the people who are as selfless as you and ask them to pay it forward to more selfless folks.*

*One person at a time, I am sure we will make the world a better place.*

*Warm Regards,*

*Chanakya*

*Email id:theseasonedshrelock@gmail.com*